this book belongs to

Surviving Your Dog's Adolescence

ALSO BY CAROL LEA BENJAMIN

Dog Training for Kids

Dog Tricks (with Captain Arthur J. Haggerty)

Dog Problems

The Wicked Stepdog, a novel

Cartooning for Kids

Nobody's Baby Now, a novel

Mother Knows Best: The Natural Way
to Train Your Dog

Writing for Kids

Second-Hand Dog: How to Turn Yours
into a First-Rate Pet

The Chosen Puppy: How to Select and Raise
a Great Puppy from an Animal Shelter

Carol Lea Benjamin

PHOTOGRAPHS BY STEPHEN LENNARD
AND CAROL LEA BENJAMIN
ILLUSTRATIONS BY CAROL LEA BENJAMIN

HOWELL BOOK HOUSE
NEW YORK

Surviving Your Dog's Adolescence

A POSITIVE TRAINING PROGRAM

MACMILLAN • USA

Macmillan General Reference
A Simon & Schuster Macmillan Company
1633 Broadway
New York, NY 10019-6785

Parts of this book were previously published in a slightly different
form in *Pure-Bred Dogs / American Kennel Gazette* in November 1985,
March 1987, September 1987, October 1988, January 1990, February
1990, March 1990, August 1990, September 1990, August 1991 and
April 1992.

Library of Congress Cataloging-in-Publication Data

Benjamin, Carol Lea.
Surviving your dog's adolescence : a positive training program /
Carol Lea Benjamin ; photographs by Stephen Lennard and Carol
Lea Benjamin ; illustrations by Carol Lea Benjamin.

   p. cm.
   Includes index.
ISBN: 0-87605-742-3
   1. Dogs—Training. 2. Dogs—Behavior. I. Title.
     SF431.B24   1993
   636.7'0887—dc20   93-17879 CIP

10 9 8

Printed in the United States of America

For Stephen, Best of Opposite Sex

And for Dexter, who taught me
how to zoom little airplanes of dog food
into his waiting mouth.
(So—you're perfect?)

I love you guys!

CONTENTS

ACKNOWLEDGMENTS

The author wishes to thank:

Gail, Steve and Alix Grossman and *Jake*, their adorable Bernese Mountain Dog;

Catherine Gorlin and Laura Calderone and *Angus*, their cute West Highland White Terrier;

William Scolnik and *Holden*, his handsome Boxer;

Polly DeMille and Richard Siegel and old friends *Benson*, the Lab mix and *Stewie*, the German Shorthaired Pointer;

Margaret McGee and *Carrie*, her much-loved Golden Retriever;

Bettiann Fishman and *Lucy*, the movie star;

Dexter, whose adolescence gave me just the right proportions of inspiration and exasperation to get me through this book

and *Scarlet*, who gave me my Ph.D. in dogs.

Alfred Grossman, DVM, 1993 president-elect of The New York State Veterinary Medical Society and owner of Murray Hill Animal Hospital in New York City, for his careful reading of the manuscript with an eye toward ensuring the health and safety of your dog, and for the warm, informed care he has always given the canine members of my family.

The American Kennel Club for allowing me a continuing forum for my thoughts and ideas about dogs.

Larry Berg, Steve Diller, Job Michael Evans and Captain Arthur Haggerty, four outstanding members of my profession who have both my admiration and affection. You guys are the greatest!

Gail Grossman, for the design of the bookplate.

Steven Bills for his careful darkroom work.

Aidan Kemp and Louise Esler, Dexter's second "parents," with a special lipsticky kiss for Steaky.

Madelyn Larsen, my editor, who keeps her own cool (and mine), who knows when to wield a blue pencil and when not to, and for her good company in both wet and dry weather.

William Reiss, my agent, for good representation for over a decade.

With hugs for Victoria and Stephen Joubert, Mimi Kahn and Dick (Legs) Goodman, Laurie and Tim Lehey and for Judy Nelson, wherever you are, honey.

And a hug for Ollie—Still missing *you*, Red.

Part One

"I don't mind a reasonable amount of trouble."

SAM SPADE IN DASHIELL HAMMETT'S
THE MALTESE FALCON

1

WHERE, OH, WHERE HAS MY LITTLE DOG GONE?

He starts out life as he always has, blind, deaf and helpless, a small, soft, furry thing whose round head, plaintive cries and sweet, milky smell elicit tenderness in adults, even some not of his species but of ours. Often, it is at this stage that his future "pack" falls hopelessly in love with him, sometimes without even knowing the skills he was genetically programmed to act out, his adult size, or his probable temperament. But how can we be blamed for falling for one of nature's best booby traps, the puppy.

Was that how our forefathers got hooked, so long ago? Was it the adorable, mewling puppy, just begging to be held, or was it instead an opportunity noted that was not to be missed: a working companion for the hunt, a low-maintenance burglar alarm and an energy-efficient heating system to warm cold tootsies at the end of a long, difficult day? Who knows? One way or another, *canis familiaris*, the world's cutest opportunist, wiggled or worked his way into the heart of man.

However the relationship began, the practical side of it was a natural. The dog had a superior sense of smell. Man had a bigger brain. Together they could work better than each was able to apart.

Even today, men and women who hunt often employ a dog as a helpmate. By now, as a result of selective breeding, the dog has become a specialist. He points, flushes, tolls, retrieves. Over the years, as man's lifestyle changed, he selectively bred dogs for other needed skills: herding, guarding, scent discrimination, scout work, tracking. Yet if modern life reveals anything about history, the impractical reasons were what made the bond solid. For while few dogs work for a living today, their place with our species is stronger than ever. The pleasures they offer us have passed the test of time.

Despite the pluses of modern dog ownership, we have problems now, problems which did not exist when this relationship began. Back then, the business of survival was pretty much of a dawn-to-dusk deal. By the time the humans were teenagers, if indeed they lived that long, they had families of their own and were

The pleasures dogs offer us have passed the test of time.

working hard to put food on the table and pelts on their bodies. No one had the leisure time in which to do or be anything like the adolescents of today. Back then, you were born, you grew up and old quickly, you worked your tail off from day one, and you died young. If you were really lucky, you had a dog by your side for all or at least part of your short, perilous journey.

The dogs back then lived differently, too. For one thing, they, too, worked their tails off, so to speak, hunting far and wide, bearing and caring for young, keeping clean and warm, offering enough affection and humor to their human partners to keep getting their contracts renewed year after year, even when the world began to change radically.

Was there ever a bratty adolescent dog back then? Hardly! First of all, the whole concept of adolescence, the bratty part of the concept as opposed to the hormonal part, requires leisure. No one had any. Period. As for the hormonal side, for humans and dogs alike, when you got your hormones, you made good use of them. There was no population explosion to worry about. In fact, enough of both species got killed just in the course of things that for either species to survive, procreation was not merely a pretty good idea, it was a must. Life was faster then. To repeat a phrase, you were born, you grew up and old quickly, you worked your tail off from day one, and you died young.

Skipping nearly all of written history, here we are today. But now, after we satisfy our urgent need for food, shelter and designer clothing, we don't have to go right to bed. We have electricity now, and central heating. We have books, and television sets. We have leisure time now, and, God help us, teenagers.

Adolescents now, free from the hunt, the farm and the sweatshop, have time to watch MTV, hang out at the mall, act up and act out. Today teenagers can define a few years of their lives, those between adorable childhood and responsible adulthood, as years during which they can make their parents regret not having used birth control more consistently. Adolescence as a stage of development *and* a state of mind is here.

Then, procreation was a must.

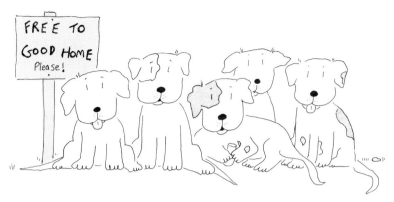

FREE TO GOOD HOME Please!

Now, we have hideous overpopulation.

But what does this have to do with dogs? They used to expend their time and energy hunting for food, raising their young, protecting their tribe. Now the working dog's a rare bird and canine unemployment is commonplace. Most dogs live in single-pet households without companionship of their own kind, alone all day with nothing to do. They, too, like many human teens, have too much energy and not enough to do. They, too, have an adolescence, both as a stage of development and a state of mind.

Look at it this way. When all this began, the growing pup developing into an adult would begin working alongside adults, just as human children did, say, in our agrarian days. When that puppy turned into an exuberant teen, he used up all his increased energy working, at least if he wanted to eat he did. If he had adolescent ants in his pants, they were gone by evening, worked out, as it were. And if not, if he needed to have a crazy fit, running around like a lunatic, just as your dog may be doing right now, he did it out of doors where there were other dogs to interact with and no vehicles to run him over. He didn't do it in a quiet living room, disturbing the family that was watching TV.

Now yesterday's affable, dependent, quiet puppy, the one who used to be content to sleep on your lap, is having crazy fits in the living room when *The Godfather* is on TV, and frankly, much as you adore him, there are times you'd like to make him an offer he can't refuse.

The trouble is that our teenaged dogs, still as natural as the day they first joined up with our kind, can't live in a natural way. They can't use up their energy hunting for dinner, nor can they simply run all day, swim whenever they like, rough and tumble any old time with others of their own kind in endless space or mate whenever the season comes around. Now we have leash laws, dangerous traffic, hideous overpopulation and massive canine unemployment. Now we have a problem.

YESTERDAY YOU WERE A HERO . . .

Unless you got an older dog, already an adolescent, you started out with a little puppy. He was tractable then. He followed you around, came when you clapped your hands, looked at you adoringly. You were his hero and that made you feel terrific. It even made all the work you had to do to take care of him well worth it.

If you began to train your puppy, by any method, he sat when told, gave his paw, walked nicely at your side. You probably house trained him. And he only chews paper now, and, once in while, steals a sock.

At that time, when your puppy was a wide-eyed visitor in a brand-new world, he was totally dependent on you, and he seemed

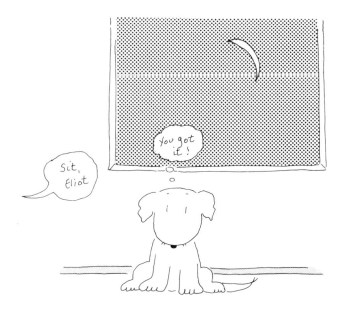

to know it. Long after his mother severed his umbilical cord with her sharp teeth and licked him vigorously to start him breathing, his psychological umbilical cord remained intact, invisible to the eye but powerful nonetheless. During his first few months with you, he wouldn't have dreamed of challenging you in any significant way. Instead, he tagged along, hoping to please, longing to bask in your favor and affection.

Then everything changed, seemingly overnight.

Canine adolescence can start as early as five months of age in small breeds and as late as nine or ten months of age in larger breeds. The bigger the dog, the slower the development, so that the giant breeds may remain adolescents until two and a half or three years of age.

In the male, adolescence usually starts with the descent of the testicles followed by scent marking. In other words, when your boy dog begins to lift his leg, he's a teen. At this time, he may become less friendly, even aggressive, toward other males. He may be more interested in roaming and less interested in obeying you. He may begin to hike his leg indoors. He may become a total brat.

In females, adolescence may be said to begin with the onset of estrus. During this three-week heat period, the bitch's vulva will

swell and there will be a bloody discharge. Though the ideal mating period is sometime during the second week, bitches have been known to accept males both early and late during their season and thus an intact female should be kept away from intact male dogs for the entire three weeks. The bitch may exhibit erratic behavior during her heat period in addition to the adolescent difficulties soon to be described. She may be moody, lethargic, even aggressive.

For pet owners trying to understand canine adolescence, attitude is far more significant than age or physical development. The aspect of adolescence that drives owners crazy is behavioral. Now that the little puppy who adored you and hung on every word is a teenager, his hormone-inspired confidence, greater strength and body size, and experience in the world are making him cocky and independent, an original thinker. To tell the truth, there are days when he could drive you nuts!

Are you starting to worry?

- Does your dog have a bit of a chewing problem?

- Does he act like a wild maniac when all you want is peace and quiet?

• Do you need your dog's permission to get into bed?

• Has his house training gone down the toilet?

• Does he ever scare you?

- Like Rodney Dangerfield, do you get no respect?

The dog you want does not just happen all by itself. You must build the dog of your dreams, slowly, carefully, with knowledge of dog behavior and training techniques, intelligent planning and an inexhaustible sense of humor. But in order to create the companion you desire, you must start with a good foundation, a dog with good character. If the dog has a poor temperament, there's no way you can make a great dog out of him. Sometimes, if the genetic clay from which your dog is made is so poor that he is wantonly aggressive, you will not even be able to make him into a suitable pet, let alone a wonderful, reliable companion. Yet without understanding your dog's nature and without having tried to train him properly, how can you know if what you see is a problem of temperament or a problem of poor communication?

I hear so many bright people blaming their dogs for their own lack of appropriate leadership. "The dog's stupid," they tell me. Or, "He's too old to learn."

Before you condemn your dog as stupid or beyond the age of education or a product of poor breeding, a hopeless thing to be destroyed, attempt to build upon the foundation you have and see what develops. Every dog deserves a chance. Most owners are utterly shocked when they begin to act appropriately and train their dogs with a method based on sound principles to see that the dog they thought was too stupid, too old or too spiteful to obey is turning into a well-mannered, enjoyable and reliable companion.

Naturally, you must be realistic in your expectations. You cannot expect a lively young terrier to behave like a geriatric sporting dog. But working with what you have, you surely can expect improvement and you can expect, as well, once you point your dog and yourself in the right direction, to help your dog become the very best dog possible for who he is. And that's a lot.

If you have problems now, or feel hopeless, cheer up. The adolescent dog is eminently trainable. Furthermore, adolescence is not only the naughtiest time of your dog's life, it is also the most exuberant time. The adolescent dog, full of energy and full of beans, can be a delightful playmate, and if you learn, by using this book, how to channel much of his energy into games, exercise and work, his adolescence will be a joyous, happy, fun time for both of you.

Once again, it's *not* too late to train or retrain your dog and help him become the appropriate companion you deserve. The skills and knowledge you will need are forthcoming, but first let's look at some of the behaviors you may expect to see in an adolescent dog. No matter how old your dog is, if he is exhibiting more than a few of the behaviors evident in the following mini case histories, he's an adolescent at heart and you will find the help you need in this book.

THE HALLMARKS
OF ADOLESCENCE

FRISKY / *Exuberance (Okay, overexuberance)*

The name of this story is "Frisky Never Sleeps." Someone up there was laughing when we named our Smooth Fox Terrier Frisky. It would not be an exaggeration to say that it is an apt name for him. Frisky is impossible to tire. The more we play with him, the more he wants to play. This is great when we feel like playing with him. But we have a few other things to do in our lives, working for a living, eating dinner and sleeping, to name a few. Frisky doesn't approve of these activities. He runs around like a maniac while we eat dinner or watch TV. He keeps dropping his toys on us when we are in bed.

Even when we take Frisky out, he pulls and pulls. And God forbid he sees another dog, you can't get him there fast enough. He's wonderfully friendly and never aggressive to other males. But he never gets tired. Sometimes we wish he'd get depressed and just lie around moping. But no. A rainy Monday morning comes around and Frisky is as cheerful and energetic as ever.

People tell us we got the wrong dog. But he's here. And frankly, we love our dog. We just have no idea how to control him. Ever.

CASPAR/ *Aggression toward people*

Five months ago I adopted the cutest puppy from our local shelter. They said they thought he was a Cocker Spaniel–Beagle mix—we call him a Speagle—but now, at eight months of age, he weighs sixty-two pounds and he's still growing. His size has never mattered because he was so good. Everyplace I went, Caspar followed me. He always came when I called or when my husband, George, whistled to him.

We wanted to do everything right so we went to puppy class with Caspar when he was three and a half months old. He was one of the best puppies in class. He learned quickly. He would do anything for a treat. He would even do his commands if we only gave him a treat once every few times, like the trainer said we should.

Caspar has always been a very affectionate dog, constantly coming over and putting his head on your lap to be petted or bringing his ball for you to throw. We've been so pleased with him. But then, all of a sudden, everything seemed to change.

When Caspar was about six and a half months old, he began to growl at us if we walked near him when he was eating. My husband said that it was natural for a dog to protect his food, so we'd put down his bowl and quickly leave the kitchen. But then he began to growl at us in the middle of the night if we rolled over in bed—he has always slept on the bed with us. And now if I hold up a treat and say, "Caspar, sit," instead of sitting, he sneezes or yawns and walks away. He won't come. One day we thought we had lost him in the park when he ran after a squirrel and then disappeared for thirty minutes. So now we can't let him off the leash and we don't know how to exercise him. I don't understand what happened to our sweet little boy.

NORMAN / *Hormonal peaks and valleys, vacillates between dependence and independence*

Remember adolescence? Remember your moods, those egomaniacal highs and suicidal lows? That's our Norman. We named him after Norman Mailer because we were told the breed was very smart. We thought Norman was a real intellectual, one of those big brain dogs that seem to understand the English language. But now we have the following scenario. One day Norman is full of energy, full of himself and impossible to reach. On days like that he doesn't seem to remember his own name, let alone anything we taught him in obedience school. The next day Norman may want to sleep all day. Worse yet, sometimes he wants to sit on my lap and sleep. We are talking about a Bernese Mountain Dog, eighty-seven pounds and still "filling out."

Sometimes when we wake up in the morning, we wonder which Norman will greet us, Norman the deaf egomaniac or Norman the napper. Sometimes, when he's acting like the Norman we used to know and love, affectionate, reasonable, bright, obedient, we wonder how *he* must feel, not knowing from day to day who he'll be when he wakes up in the morning. People in the breed tell us not to worry, he'll be super when he grows up. They say he'll be grown up when he's three years old. What are we supposed to do for the two years and four months until that happens?

LESLIE / *Shyness or fearfulness*

Leslie always loved kids but all of a sudden, at eight months of age, she began to freak whenever she saw a kid coming toward her. I try to get the kid to pet her or feed her something, but if I make her stay near the kid, she just starts shaking. No kid has ever hurt her. I don't get it.

SPIRIT / *Fussy eating and erratic appetite*

My female Shepherd, Spirit, was never a good eater, even as a growing puppy, but now, it's the pits. First she began going off food. We'd change the food. We'd add little goodies.

Eventually my wife began to cook special dog soups to put on top of the dry food. I'd come home and say, "Wow, it sure smells good in here," and she'd say, "Forget about it. It's Spirit's soup." Well, Spirit liked the soup. But if you left the kitchen, she'd stop eating and follow you. So my wife would stay in the kitchen until Spirit finished eating. But then, even with my wife there, Spirit would stop eating and go look for me. So then my wife would say, "What are you going to do, let the dog *starve*?" So then I stood in the kitchen, too. We'd lean on the counter and while she ate we had to say stuff like "Good girl, yummy, yummy." Spirit would eat and wag her tail. Why not? She had us right where she wanted us. But then sometimes even with the soup and with us there, she wouldn't eat, so then my wife would stick her hand in the disgusting mix of dog food and warm soup and Spirit would daintily eat her meal off my wife's hand. This is where we are now. I shudder to think of what will come next.

ARNOLD / *Brute force*

You have to understand. Arnold, our Mastiff, is the sweetest dog in the world. He wouldn't hurt a fly. He just doesn't know his own strength. Sometimes he's okay, I mean, when he doesn't see anything that interests him. But God help your arm if he sees a dog he wants to play with or a person he knows will pet him. Even in the house, I end up with a black and blue mark every time Arnold turns around. Is there any way a dog can learn not to smash into you with the force of a bulldozer?

PRINCESS / *Inability to resist temptation*

Princess, as the saying goes, can resist anything but temptation. She also has the broadest definition of temptation I've ever run across. Naturally, forget leaving food anywhere in the house. She's like a cat and can even get up on the kitchen counters if it seems worth her while, spelled f-o-o-d. But she also can't resist socks, even when they're on your feet, the belt of a bathrobe, paper from the waste-paper basket, my eyeglass case, makeup, anything with a little tear or a thread hanging from it, knitted things like sweaters, and, it goes without saying, shoes.

Princess is terrific at her obedience commands indoors, if you don't ask her to stay too long, but take her out and let her see another dog and she doesn't know you're still on earth with her. Nor does she care. Will this dog ever shape up?

LOUIS / *Inappropriate protectiveness*

My roommate and I got a Doberman because we live in an iffy neighborhood and we figured no one would bother the house with Louis there or us when Louis was with us. Louis started barking at the door when he was four months old and we always praised him for doing so. He was very alert, even barking when someone passed the apartment on the way to another one down the hall. He made us feel very safe. A little later on, when he was five and a half months old, Louis began growling if we opened the door for someone he didn't know. We never knew Dobermans were so smart or that Louis would practically train himself but he sure was doing just that. So we'd praise him for protecting us and after a minute or so, we could let the person in.

When Louis was six and a half months old, he began growling at strangers in the street. Gary and I would always try to calm him down, petting him and talking softly to him, but instead of calming him down, he got worse. Now he's lunging at people and we have to be very careful when we walk him. I've started taking him out odd hours, when fewer people are around, and very late at night. And we can't really have any friends over. We don't want to ruin Louis's protective instinct by punishing him for keeping us safe, but he seems to be getting sort of *too* protective, if you know what I mean. We don't know how to have him be a friendly normal dog and still protect us when there's danger.

LINDA / *Obedience burnout, selective deafness*

I just want to know why my yellow Lab doesn't seem to *hear* me when I call her, but if you open the refrigerator or start to prepare food, boom, she's there. When she was a little puppy, if

I just squeaked a squeak toy at her or whistled, she'd come running. Now I find it difficult to get her attention. Her mind always seems to be elsewhere, like out to lunch. I heard this breed is very obedient. You could fool me!

Look, Linda is only eleven months old and we'd like her to learn more stuff, but we can't seem to teach her anything anymore. She's all lively and animated when we play, but the minute we get her leash and ask her to actually do something for us, she looks depressed, like she's too sad or too tired to do her lesson. Is she too old to learn anything new, or what?

WALLY / *Slow learner, fast forgetter*

When Wally, my Airedale, was little, he seemed to want to please and he always came when called. He learned everything very quickly, you know, sit, give your paw, not going to the bathroom in the house. Everything.

Now Wally seems to be forgetting at a faster rate than he is learning. Even when he "gets it," it takes him so long he seems, well, dense. By the next day, you give the same command he finally got the day before and you might as well be speaking Chinese. You just have to start all over from scratch.

ELIZABETH / *Grooming problems*

Elizabeth would rather die than have her nails cut. If she sees the clipper, she runs away. If you try to force her to have her nails cut, she growls. One time she even snapped at me and sort of grabbed my hand. I know she didn't mean to hurt me, but I don't cut her nails anymore.

FAIRBANKS / *Destructiveness*

Fairbanks, our Malamute, is in the process of destroying his second couch. One day, when he was seven months old, I came home to find a huge hole in one of the couch pillows, like he was trying to bury his bone there. After that, he didn't touch anything for six weeks, except maybe a shoe or some underwear. You don't want to know what I came home to then. Suffice it to say, I ordered a new couch. I thought chewing was something dogs did when they were teething, but, trust me, Fairbanks has his adult teeth. Big ones. Now an arm of the new couch is sort of missing and, on top of that, Fairbanks looks like he's going bald. He's sort of molting all over the house. This is not exactly what I had in mind when I bought the cutest puppy you ever saw at the mall.

TOFU / *Aggression to other dogs*

Tofu, our Akita, was very well socialized as a puppy, the breeder told us this was very important, and he loved to play with other dogs. We thought it would always be like that, but when he reached eight months of age, he began lifting his leg when he urinated and shortly after that, he began growling at other dogs, even dogs he used to play with on a regular basis.

At first we could let Tofu play with females and he was okay. He'd sniff them a lot, but he wouldn't growl or fight. But then he began to get aggressive with females, too. Now we can't take him to the play group in the park anymore, and when we see someone else approaching with a dog, we have to get out of the way and hold Tofu's mouth shut. One of our friends suggested he was angry because he didn't like his name and the vet says to neuter him, but he won't guarantee that that will stop Tofu's aggression toward other dogs. We had wanted to breed him. Now we don't know *what* to do.

E.T. / *Bossy, manipulative, always testing*

Our mutt, E.T., short for Ersatz Terrier, is the bossiest dog I've ever met. He's so cheeky, when I give him a command, he barks back at me. In the evening, when I want to read, E.T. tosses his ball onto my lap, backs up and starts barking. I know it's probably bad, but I usually throw the ball for him. I don't know what else to do when he barks like that.

That part's the easy stuff. What I can't stand is that after he learns to do things, you ask him to do them again and he won't. He just sits and stares at me when I call him to come or ask him to lie down. Even sometimes when I go to put on his leash to take him out, he keeps moving his head away like it's all some kind of big joke. I guess he has more time on his hands than I do, because sometimes his little games make me late for work and I get very upset at him. Still, he's a great dog. I just wish he'd let *me* be the boss.

MARLON / *Housebreaking problems*

Marlon *was* house trained. In fact, like most Basenjis, he is a very clean, almost catlike dog. But shortly after he started lifting his leg, Marlon began to take his new skill too seriously. I could cope with him occasionally washing down a table leg or (his favorite) the umbrella stand. At least they're easy to clean. But one day, right after my husband came home from a business trip, Marlon began peeing on Warren's side of the bed, usually on his pillow. This we do not like. I began to use the crate again, figuring that maybe I went too fast and he didn't really get it. So then Marlon would lift his leg and pee through the wire side of the crate so that he still had someplace dry to lie down. He can be very dear and he's the funniest dog we ever met, but sometimes I feel like strangling him. There's this woman down the street from us with three Basenjis. How does she do it?

LUCILLE / *Unreliable*

Lucille, my American Staffordshire Terrier, always stayed pretty close to me when she was a puppy and she always came when I called her. Because of that, I felt it was okay to take her off leash in the park. But last week, two days after her eighth-month birthday, Lucille was playing with a young male dog and suddenly they took off and ran away. I called and called, but she wouldn't come. They went out of sight and I didn't see Lucille again for twenty minutes. Let me tell you, I was *frantic* and until I solve this problem, Lucille is staying on leash.

Caspar, the "Speagle," has become aggressive. Fairbanks, the Malamute, has set out for China, straight down through the living room couch. Linda, the yellow Lab, goes deaf when her owner calls her to come, but she can still hear the sound of the can opener from three rooms away. Frisky, the Smooth Fox Terrier, has crazy fits when his owners try to watch television. He looks as if he's doing an imitation of a tornado and nothing they have tried will slow him down. Spirit, the Shepherd, only eats out of her "mother's" hand. And Marlon, the Basenji, has begun urinating on his "dad's" side of the bed.

What can you do when the adorable puppy who followed you around the house, licked your hand submissively and *always* came when called turns into a brassy brat with a major attitude? Worse still, what can you do if you've already been to a training class or read a couple of dog books and the techniques that seemed to work pretty well on your puppy no longer work on your growing dog?

You might think an older student, a half-grown dog, would be easier to train than a baby puppy? How long, after all, can a puppy concentrate? How much can one absorb?

Remember junior high? Remember anything you learned there?

But I bet you remember grade school, even the names of your favorite teachers. The truth is that young puppies, eight or nine or ten weeks old, have a wonderful ability to concentrate, to focus on the teacher and to ignore other stimuli, for short periods of time. Interestingly enough, during those short periods in which you can teach an amazing amount, a bit at a time, they are less distractable than adolescent dogs. On the other hand, adolescent dogs are distracted by everything. In fact, they are distracted when there is nothing visible or auditory around to distract them. They are distracted, perhaps, by their own changing bodies.

The little puppy who just followed his mother's bidding will easily switch that respect, that biddability, to you. He's eager to please you, easy to lead, willing—and able—to learn, curious about his surroundings. His very dependence upon you makes him pay attention to you and try as hard as he can to do as you say.

Almost any method of training will work on a little puppy, as long as you are gentle, work consistently, keep your lessons short and sweet.

The adolescent dog, a resident of Hormone City, is a horse of another color. He's feeling independent for the first time in his life and he wants to test the limits of his freedom. Why should he follow you when he could follow his own path? And, anyway, what are you going to do about it if he *doesn't* listen?

Perhaps the dog, like the person, cannot grow up without some kind of testing, finding out by trial and error who he is and what he is capable of. Now the world attracts his attention the way his mother once did, and then you did. Now his mind is no longer occupied by one thing, but by many things. His interests are wider. And as for being eager to please, he is. But it is himself he most wants to please nowadays.

He's a free thinker, no more is he mama's little puppy. He's bigger, too, and stronger. Maybe he even wants to see if *he* can be the leader now. After all, adolescence is a time of experimentation, of testing.

Treats won't hold his attention now, the way they could have when he was a puppy. Anyway, he's well fed, isn't he? So unless you care to *starve* him before trying to educate him, why should he care about tidbits? Half the time he couldn't care less about food, even at mealtime. There are more interesting things in the wind now that he's an adolescent. (Remember?)

Still, in a way, you can expect more during a lesson from a bigger, more mature dog than from a puppy. Certainly the adolescent has the stamina for a longer training lesson, but will you? Just keeping his attention can wear you out! It is far easier to start with a little puppy, and if your training method is one that has lifelong efficacy, such as the one used in this book, you will have already handled many of the issues that become difficult in adolescence before those hormones hit. You probably will have to do a lot of reminding, but that's a whole lot easier than starting from scratch.

It is himself he most wants to please nowadays.

Dogs are trainable at any age: Ben, 8½ years, Stewie, 7 years, Dexter, 10 months, Scarlet, 9 years.

If you are more or less starting from go with your adolescent, don't fret. Dog are trainable at any age. And while the adolescent will tax your patience, keep in mind that he's also a lot of fun. Adolescence is a time of unbridled energy. The adolescent dog sees the world as someplace fresh, new and wonderful. This is good. This can help you to see and enjoy things anew, seeing the world through dog-colored glasses. You may not believe this when you're tired and want to be left alone or when you just want your dog to behave properly, but several of the behaviors typical of adolescent dogs have a plus side as well as a minus side. Others will be outgrown. Nearly all can be worked with or around.

It's the philosophy of this book to turn every possible aspect of adolescence into a plus and find constructive and pleasurable ways to train, play with and enjoy the exuberant teenage canine, even if now he appears to look like a full-blown juvenile delinquent.

With any luck, your dog will not exhibit all these behaviors, or, if he does, he won't exhibit all of them all the time. But even if he does, all these behaviors will be addressed in this book, and only one, aggression, should give you any cause for concern. Even in that case, there are solutions that work for many dogs.

You may wonder how your dog will react to all the changes you will be making in order to teach him and eliminate his behavior problems. Most dogs react initially with great interest and curiosity. They like new stuff to do. They love the attention. They even seem to like learning. Soon enough, or shall I say, too soon, they figure out they are losing control. They still like getting your attention and time. But many dogs at this stage try disobedience as an interesting alternative to the ready compliance you are after. Each dog attempts to get out of work in his or her own style— some play deaf or dumb, some get too busy to listen, some get sleepy, some get aggressive and try to scare you off. There'll be a lot more about this later on. For now, I am happy to report that if you proceed along in a matter-of-fact fashion, your dog will proceed to a third stage. He will come to enjoy being a reasonably obedient dog and getting lots of positive attention for his effort.

How about the effect all the changes will have on you? Years ago, a psychiatrist told me that she believed most of her patients would prefer to mail in their checks and skip their therapy sessions. Change is painful. Even when you are getting glorious results for your effort—a wonderfully trained dog who pays attention to you and adores you all the more for taking charge—you may still find the changes you have to make stressful at first. But like your dog, if you stick with the program, you will absorb the changes and be glad you took this route. After all, a happy, trained pet dog is always more of a pleasure than a disgruntled brat who pays you no mind.

What if you are one of the rare owners of an adolescent dog who has no problems, who doesn't find his dog in any of the case histories above? Read on anyway. This book can still show you how to build a better dog. It is full of suggestions for silly and enjoyable yet educational games that will enable you to have more fun with your dog, gain deeper understanding and, over time, help him become the dog you've always wanted. So don't bemoan the end of puppyhood. When you ask yourself, "Where, oh, where has my little dog gone?" the answer is that he has become a zestful, playful, exuberant adolescent and, with the help of this book, you're going to make him the very best adolescent dog he can be.

Before we go on to learn the most important lesson, how to win your dog's respect, let's take a quick look at the world as your dog sees it. Learning to think like a dog will help you appreciate

Your dog is not a little person in fur.

your dog as a dog and, ultimately, it will help you train him. You may find this list of dog laws funny, but after you laugh, think about what each law really means. Dogs don't use their senses in the same way we do, nor do they communicate with words as we do. Dogs often communicate with their urine or feces, a fact every owner of an adolescent dog should understand. And last, as you take a peek at how your dog views things, I hope you are reminded that your dog is not a little person in fur. He is as different from you and me as an extraterrestrial might be. This makes it all the more amazing and wonderful that we can learn to communicate with each other and, more than that, be true companions and friends.

DOG LAWS

The Laws of Nature from a Dog's Point of View

Dog Law 1: **Examine everything:**
      a. Smell it.
      b. Taste it.

(continued on next page)

(continued from previous page)

       c. Play with it.

       d. If possible, ingest it.

       e. If all else fails, urinate on it.

Dog Law 2: Anything (or anyone) on the floor is fair game.

Dog Law 3: Whenever possible, move up in the pecking order.

Dog Law 4: Observe humans carefully (they have the can openers).

Dog Law 5: DOGS ONLY: If it sticks up, has been marked, if you like it, if you don't like it, if you want it, if you don't know what it is, if it scared you (and so on), mark it; if it's nice, mark it twice.

Dog Law 6: BITCHES ONLY: If it's male, tease it; if it responds, show your teeth, snap and act indignant.

Dog Law 7: The Canfield Law: Never miss an opportunity to eat or go to the bathroom.

Dog Law 8: Ollie's Law: A little nap never hurt anyone.

2

WINNING YOUR DOG'S RESPECT

As a pack animal, bred and born for cooperative living, the dog is the great communicator. It is a dog's very nature to be able to assess a group of any species to determine strong from weak, alpha from omega, and, clever thing, to place himself accurately in the hierarchy. He does this by using and reading body language, facial expression and tone of voice, the subtle signs and signals of natural authority or the lack of it.

Body language is ritualized; each posture, gesture or grimace has a set meaning. The play bow executed by a Pug can be understood by a Whippet, a Doberman or, for that matter, a wolf. In fact, if *you* imitate any of this natural language, your dog will almost certainly respond. He can understand your play bow as an invitation to play as easily as if it were delivered by the Cocker Spaniel next door.

Body language is ritualized. The play bow is an invitation to a romp. Dexter understands, and responds.

He reads the feeling behind the posture, too.

Even though it's a first date, he allows a kiss!

Your dog can do much more than interpret the body language of his own and related species, even as imitated by a human. He can also determine from your stance how seriously you mean what you say. The more you appear to be in charge, the more quickly he'll shape up and do what's requested of him. If you are having trouble getting him to come close, bending down, even extending your arms out to the side is an invitation he can easily read but not easily resist. So using body language is not simply a matter of learning how to look tougher, it's a matter of understanding what signal would be appropriate at the moment and taking advantage of that knowledge to communicate more precisely to your dog.

The facial expressions of dogs change according to mood, as with humans. Your dog can distinguish between a friendly expression and a threatening one, no matter if the other party is his owner or another dog. Sometimes your facial expression alone, with a dog who has been taught to take real notice of you, can serve as praise or correction.

Although dogs can't speak our language, they do use and understand a variety of sounds. Mother dogs will use a deeper tone of voice to warn or correct and a higher pitched tone to show approval. Puppies, from the time they can hear, know one tone from

Facial expressions change according to mood.

another. So if your dog cringes when you yell at him for yet another accident on the rug, but doesn't seem to *learn*, it's not spite. It simply means when you yell, he knows you're angry at him. But untrained, he may not know why. Untrained, he has not

made the leap to listening carefully to *our* language and eventually learning what some key words mean. He has not learned, unless you have taught him, how to concentrate and put two and two together in a language he was not born to understand. Nonetheless, he is capable of learning our way of communicating too, at least to a degree. As you work with him, his understanding will improve. But before you expect *him* to become bilingual, you should make the leap yourself, learning to both understand and use *his* ways of communicating. It is, in part, by doing this that you will win his respect. Understanding canine body language, tone and facial expression will help you see the subtle signs of challenge or the evidence that your dog is treating you as a litter mate or equal and not as his leader. You can also gain an edge and add efficiency to your training program by making intelligent use of body language yourself, standing tall when you are training, crouching when you want to play or entice your dog to come quickly to you. You will know that, once you have gotten your dog's attention, a look can be a powerful message. And you will know how to pitch your voice so that your dog will take you seriously, hearing by your tone of voice whether it's time for work or play.

What happens when the dog finds out someone other than he merits leadership? Were he human, he might become small and bitter, full of thoughts of revenge. But he's not human. Isn't that partly why we are so attached to his species? He feels no resentment at all. Instead, and here's the kicker, he worships the one he recognizes as worthy of leadership, the *alpha*. There is nothing more attractive to a dog than his alpha.

Did your dog ever instantly offer the crown to a stranger? In a living room full of company, did he choose a particular person to look at with his own special combination of adoration and respect? Observing this will clearly demonstrate how swiftly and accurately dogs make these decisions and how deliciously attractive, how irresistible the leader of the pack is to a dog. There's a kind of mental strength and greatness of spirit that any dog can recognize and respond to. It is what makes him feel safe and happy. It is the right of every dog to know who's in charge.

If you fear that being "dominant" over your dog will lose you his love, or if you have been taught that leadership is unnecessary or even unkind, you may suffer from a serious misunderstanding of the nature of the dog. The happiest dog will have a leader, an alpha figure he can respect and adore. It is from this hierarchy that he draws his security, his sense of belonging, his sense of place.

Winning your dog's respect, a feat that can be accomplished in a quiet, gentle, even graceful manner, gives him the most important resource of his life—someone to look up to. *You* may not feel you need a model of behavior in your life, a mentor, a problem solver, a nourisher. But you are a human adult. Your dog, because he is a dog and because he has been domesticated and lives with another species, will always be like a child. He cannot be an autonomous creature, living on his own and making important decisions for and by himself. He needs both protection and guidance. And, as you will soon discover, first by reading and then by seeing remarkable changes in your own dog, follow the leader is a serious game your dog was born to play. He is superbly well equipped to do his part.

ON BECOMING ALPHA

Alpha is an attitude, confidence brought on by understanding dogs and loving them as well. It has nothing to do with cruelty or dog abuse. It is a natural way to communicate with a dog, to teach him and to win his respect. When working with your dog in this traditional way, the way his mother taught him, you keep his focus on the relationship. This not only leads to a most satisfying friendship with a dog, its efficacy is lifelong. When your dog begins to think the dark thoughts of adolescence, "Hey, this is America. Just because you call doesn't mean I have to come," you need an appropriate relationship or language to fall back on.

No matter what stage he's going through, no matter how his hormones are fluctuating, no matter how much he feels he knows it all and can call the shots, your dog can understand the hierarchy of his mixed species family and what it requires of him. Dogs who live as family members need the natural family structure they are born to understand. To rob them of this birthright may not only result in a dog who is insecure, it may also result in a dog who is a bossy, cheeky, disobedient, sometimes belligerent, obnoxious pest.

Yet in the past few years, two unfortunate trends have gained popularity in dealing with dogs. One is the proliferation of "puppy trainers" who only deal with dogs up to the age of five months. This period, as we know, is prior to the onset of adolescence with its many annoying behavior problems. If these trainers have not worked extensively with adolescent and adult dogs, they may be inadvertently leading owners and their dogs in the wrong direction. It is by understanding full-blown aggression, to use the most difficult example, that you know precisely how to teach owners how to prevent it. It is not only what you do that counts, it is also knowing what not to do. As you will soon see, a game, a way of relating and, most importantly, a style of training, that seems fine with a small puppy may bode ill for the time when that puppy becomes an adolescent or an adult. It is fine to specialize in training puppies if you are truly experienced with all the stages that follow puppyhood. Then, what you teach and advise will be appropriate for the life of the dog, not just the puppy.

The second trend I take exception to is the use of food lures and rewards for basic training. Even though most training involves a combination of positive and negative reinforcements, praise for behavior you want repeated and a correction for behavior you wanted stopped, many "foodies" claim their training is "all positive." However lovely being "all positive" sounds, the fact is that food training falls apart when the dog hits adolescence (or, more accurately, when adolescence hits the dog!). And when you call your "positive" trainer to get help with your dog's problems, you will positively be sent to someone "who specializes in problems." If you follow the methods for training and problem correction in this book, humane and effective techniques based on the very way your dog's mother taught him the first lessons of his life, you will not have to switch methodologies should a problem arise.

It is not only what you do that counts. You also need to know what not to do.

You are dealing with a highly intelligent creature.

Traditional training, which assumes intelligence on the part of both the teacher and the student, works. It works on puppies, on adolescents, on adults—even those dogs who have been abused. So use it with confidence. This trainer will not have to apologize in midstream and send you off to find another style of dog training because the methods taught in this program are *truly* positive, *positive* meaning *clear, precise, sure, unequivocal.*

As your dog's trainer, you must recognize the difference between conditioning a dog to "perform" an unconscious "act," such as salivating, and conditioning a dog to obey a command, such as sit, which, despite conditioning, he can *choose* to ignore at any time. We are not dealing with pea-brained pigeons here but instead with highly intelligent dogs. Conditioning or shaping, traditionally done with birds and rodents, does not eliminate the dog's ability to think things through and make decisions. When temptation woos your dog, he is still able to decide that it is more attractive than your food treat.

Most important, food training tends to sidestep the issue of alpha. This may appeal greatly to people who feel they are soft rather than forceful, but it does not take a bulldozer to become alpha to a pet dog. It takes intelligence, consistency and a humane and effective training program. Sadly, those who call themselves "positive" trainers not only think little of canine intelligence, they also demean the intelligence of owners. They do not believe that the average pet owner can earn his dog's respect. Almost all my clients have been "average pet owners." All have learned how to take charge in the most humane fashion, succeeding in making their dogs secure, happily obedient, more attentive and playful companions. Every time I work with someone new, I feel sure that they will learn at least as well as their dog will! I am rarely disappointed.

I am not, however, against the use of food lures and food rewards for trick work, tracking or advanced obedience training, in other words, for performance rather than basic education, once the owner has established him or herself as the dog's leader. Yet, even in these cases, food should be phased out early on. Those who use it usually say they phase it out early but all too often get stuck with it and use it for the life of the dog. It becomes a crutch they are afraid to eliminate. The worst problem with that is that the dog knows when you are addressing him with confidence and when you are afraid he won't do something without a goodie. Dogs simply do not respect anyone who has to resort to begging and bribery. They're just too smart.

Natural dog training, training based on the efficient way dogs teach each other, puts the owner comfortably in charge. The good news is that anyone, absolutely anyone, can learn how to win his dog's respect in this way. Everyone can learn how to teach his dog a few essential commands that will safeguard the life of the dog and the sanity of the owner. Over the years, I have worked with children as young as nine or ten and successfully taught them how to project to their pet dog that they were in charge. A clear, easy program to teach you the skills you need is coming up shortly.

You may still be wondering what's wrong with omitting the concept of alpha. What if you just don't like the idea of "being in charge"?

Without a leader, what is the dog—your equal? He is hardly equipped to make decisions for his own health and well-being. You have to make decisions about his diet, medical care and grooming. You have to make decisions about what is safe for him and what isn't. He has to go along with what you decide because you are who you are, not because he understands the consequences.

Dogs who consider themselves equal to their owners rapidly become problem dogs. Trying to rise to the highest level is part of being a dog. So it is a hop, skip and a jump from equal to superior and the dog who has convinced himself that he is his owner's better quickly becomes bossy and unmanageable.

An adolescent dog without a leader is often an accident waiting to happen. In the chaotic world of hormone fluctuations, you are your dog's anchor. He must have limits. He must acquire manners. He does not, as an adolescent, have the self-control to keep himself, or those around him, safe. And since adolescence is a time of terrible insecurity, a time of heedless confidence and boundless, sudden fear, he must have someone to reflect reality for him and make him feel secure. That someone is his "alpha."

Recently I worked with a handsome, medium-sized mixed-breed adolescent dog named Roger who was showing serious signs of aggression. Roger lunged at nearly everything that moved, both indoors and out. He had already bitten once and his owner was terrified he'd do it again.

Roger was brought to me in a head halter, which his owner had been told to use to restrain him from lungeing at people. As I always do, I asked Susan to show me what the dog did for her. (They had already been through a group obedience class before calling me.) Susan told Roger to heel and began to walk. The dog was to her left, but not in the correct heel position. More importantly, he paid her no attention. He turned his head constantly and looked around frantically. When I asked to see a sit-stay, I saw more frantic behavior, as if the dog had to check out everything visible for possible danger. Needless to say, he didn't hold the stay and when he broke, Susan did not correct him. Instead, she looked at me helplessly and shrugged her shoulders as if to say, "See. He's hopeless."

Later, on a busy street, I saw Roger in all his glory, lungeing aggressively at joggers, children, just about anyone coming near him. Roger appeared to have many problems, but, in fact, he only had one—no leader. He felt responsible for checking out everything around, and most of what he saw frightened him. True, Roger was not a well-bred, calm, steady, solid, easygoing dog. Worse than that, he had no alpha in his life and felt he was in charge.

Fixing Roger's problem meant fixing the relationship. That meant convincing Susan first of all that she deserved his respect and second that, with my help, she would be able to project that message clearly to Roger. You will never convince a dog to respect you if you don't at least *act* worthy of his respect. With new skills, a nylon training collar and time to practice with encouragement and support from a trainer, Susan gradually convinced herself and then Roger that she was in charge of their little group. As Susan's self-esteem and confidence grew along with her understanding and her skills, the change in both of them was wonderful to see. Susan began to stand straighter, to use her voice more assertively, to pet and praise Roger with real oomph and, when necessary, to tell him "No," as if she meant it. Roger began to watch Susan as they walked together. The more his attention was on Susan, the less he noticed anyone else moving near him. Now Roger's greatest concern was to watch and please Susan. This was easy to do. As he performed the basic commands for her, she praised him lavishly. Roger became more steady and calm as the weeks passed. But our work was not over yet.

Now we needed to monitor Roger as he related to others. Sometimes when we'd see a child walking down the street, we'd have Roger do a sit-stay. Now he would. Because he was secure in his respect for Susan, he simply looked toward the child and sniffed the air with interest. For his nonaggressive interest, he got nicely praised. In a low-key fashion, we continued to praise Roger when he showed pleasant interest in passersby. We also were able to correct him for lungeing. I even asked my husband to join us for one lesson and run back and forth in front of Roger, hooting like a crazy person as he ran. This setup gave me a chance to show Susan how to make a good leash correction and even how to use her voice correctly when letting Roger know a certain behavior was not allowed.

Once Roger learned to trust and look to his mistress, he was a changed dog. The more he focused on Susan, the more he was able to let go of looking for things that spooked or threatened him. He finally understood, as did Susan, the function of alpha as teacher and protector.

When you go out and about with your dog, his safety is in your hands. He has to know that you will not lead him into danger, a trust that builds as you humanely train him. You have to know that when you call, your dog will not find another dog, a flock of pigeons or something blowing in the wind more attractive than you. The only way to prepare a dog for real life is by being alpha, which to me has always meant being the kindest, smartest, most fun leader you can possibly be. It is this natural type of training that goes deep, teaching a dog so well that he understands exactly what you want and happily gives it to you because (a), you are his leader and he worships you and (b), he knows you can make him do it in the same comprehensible way his mother would have should he decide it's his constitutional right to disobey.

If you're having problems with your adolescent dog, a problem with the relationship is probably at the root of your troubles. You already *know* what can happen when you're not in charge . . .

His housebreaking is a little iffy. He goes outside *if* he feels like it. He goes inside *if* he feels like it. His recall isn't reliable. Sometimes he comes when you call him, but sometimes he doesn't.

His stays are short, his attention span shorter. Worse than that, he sits and stares at you, preferably from a place where he can look down at you.

He campaigns for attention when you're reading or on the phone, and he usually gets what he wants. When you give a command, he may bark back, or worse, snap at you. He acts as if he's more important than you are. Sometimes you think about placing him elsewhere.

You think you have a lot of problems. Relax, you only have one. Your dog is alpha. You're not.

Alpha. Here lies the key to human–canine relationships. With it, you have a friend for life. Without it, you have a chronic headache. So if you think your dog thinks he's on top, he probably is. Happily, the next chapter will show you *exactly* what you can do about it.

3

HOW TO HAVE AN APPROPRIATE RELATIONSHIP WITH YOUR DOG

A TRAINER'S DOZEN FOR WINNING YOUR DOG'S RESPECT

1. Use the Body Language and Voice of Leadership

You can, and should, learn a lot from your own dog and other dogs. When dogs want to appear in charge, they rise up onto their toes to look bigger. They use their eyes assertively, their voices, too. When dogs play, they bow down to each other, their eyes twinkle, their ears go back, they wiggle and physically express friendliness and joy.

When you want to teach your dog something or command him to do something, stand tall, deepen your voice (lower, *not* louder), look seriously at your dog. When you want to play, do as your dog does, crouch down, talk in a higher voice, show your humor and friendliness in your eyes.

Your dog will respond to your posture, mood, tone of voice. Ultimately, I like my dogs trained so well that if I lie flat on the floor and say, "Down," they will lie down, too. But I do not begin training a dog by lying down on the floor! I begin by taking advantage of the dog's ability to read body language. I stand up. I speak softly but seriously. I do not repeat myself again and again. I do not shout at any dogs. Shouting reveals a lack of confidence. It is the dog's job to watch me, listen to me and to pay attention during a lesson. When I want to break a command, I bend and call the dog to me. This works, even the first day. As I proceed with any dog's education, I stretch what I can do in all directions. I begin to sit after giving a command. I increase the time I want the dog to "work." I use hand signals without verbal commands when I want to increase attentiveness. Each step of the way I am aware of what my posture and tone communicate to the dog.

2. Teach and Tighten All Basic Obedience Commands

Every dog needs obedience training for his safety and your sanity. Even a three-pound dog has a brain and needs a chance to use it. Even a three-pound dog can become a Napoleon if he is left untutored. (Instructions for basic training are in chapter 7.)

As you proceed in your training program, raise your expectations of your dog. If he takes his sweet old time to lie down when you say down, correct him immediately after you give the command. Never repeat a command. He must obey the first and only time you give it. Correct him if he doesn't. Expect and work for snappy obedience—quick response, good eye contact, straight sits, sharp heeling, all done with a wagging tail. With an adolescent dog, keep practice sessions brief and always reward good work with exercise and game playing.

3. Praise and Correct Appropriately

More than anything, it is how you praise that makes the dog want to give you the world. Praise should be given immediately for an action you want repeated or for a proper response. It should

Praise with your warm hands and your warm voice.

be delivered with authority, warmth and brevity. Don't fawn, linger, overpraise or forget that you are in the middle of a training session. If you are using food rewards, now is the time to eliminate them completely. Praise with your warm hands and your warm voice. Praise should not make the dog wild or interrupt the flow of work in any other way.

A correction *should* interrupt what is happening. That is the point of it. Correct swiftly, fairly and with oomph.

Do not undercorrect, tugging, tugging, tugging at your dog's neck because your corrections cause no change in his behavior. That's nagging and, just as a human would, your dog will learn to ignore it. But don't go to the other extreme and use an atom bomb to correct lagging. You are trying to teach, not abuse. Here's the guideline: The mildest correction *that works* is the perfect one to use. When you can *encourage* a good response, you need not correct at all.

4. Use the Long Down Once or Twice a Day

Within a week of teaching the down-stay command (see chapter 7 for instructions), work your dog up to a thirty-minute down. By the end of the second week, he should be able to do an hour

You can correct with a quick pop followed by an immediate release.

down-stay. The dog should be placed in the middle of a room, not leaning on a piece of furniture. The owner should remain in the room. After the first break, do not repeat the command. Simply go to the dog, place him back where he was with a firm leash correction and walk away. Laying the leash over the dog's back reminds him he is working and thus helps him keep the stay. This nonviolent control exercise lets the dog know that *you* are in charge.

5. Teach and Use the Emergency Down

To teach this important command, while out heeling with your dog, suddenly lower your voice to an urgent whisper. Say "Down," bend forward, slide your hand into your dog's collar, lock your elbow and push your dog straight down until he's lying on the sidewalk. This is not a stay. Praise immediately and tell him to heel. Do three of these within a few minutes and only practice three at a time, two to three times a week. After two

As soon as he's lying down, praise him . . .

then say "Heel" and immediately continue on your way.

weeks, try the voice command only, but continue to bend and use the same hand that grasped the collar to give the down signal. If your dog fails to drop immediately, without thinking it over, your hand is right there to instantly grab his leash and pull it downward. Praise. Heel. Once your dog drops instantly to your urgent command of "Down," you can begin to use it, also infrequently, when the dog is loose in the house and after that works, loose outdoors.

Teaching the emergency down is important for your dog's safety. It is the best tool for stopping him on a dime should danger loom. (I twice saved the life of my Golden Retriever, Oliver, by using this command.) But in this context, it has another value. It teaches the dog that he must obey you without thinking. For the dog who thinks he is holier than thou, this is an excellent comeuppance.

6. Work Silently

At least once a week, give your dog a good, solid review of all his training on hand signals only. *No cheating*! If he fails to notice your hand signal, use a snappy leash correction. Trust me—he'll look next time. Silent work elevates the level of training. It forces your dog to look at you and to pay attention.

7. Teach Yourself to Have Alpha Eyes

Think about how your dog sometimes stares at you, the little devil. Now try this. Next time the dog acts up in any way and you are annoyed, put him on a sit-stay and stare down at him. Feel your authority and project it through your eyes. Keep staring *until the dog breaks eye contact and looks away*. The one who holds the eye contact longest is alpha.

If this seems awkward or difficult, think about this: When you are reading and look up and see this dog you adore across the room, doesn't the dog "read" love in your eyes and wag his tail or even come to you for petting? So you are already sending messages with your eyes.

Dogs are adept at sending and receiving via the eye. But so are people. Without thinking about it, we do it all the time. You can learn to harness your assertiveness as well as your affection and project either to your dog.

8. Learn a Little Basic Wolf

For wolves, as well as dogs, the signs and signals of hierarchy are ritualized. There are no separate languages or even dialects

which would prevent a wolf or dog from Canada from understanding one from the United States.

When two wolves meet, the more dominant wolf will reaffirm
his leadership. He may do this by taking the muzzle of the subordinate wolf in his mouth. Mother dogs do this to their puppies as
well, and lest you think it's a violent or unpleasant ritual, every
puppy I have ever raised has poked his head repeatedly into the
mouth of my older dog. Knowing who is in charge gives a dog
delicious security.

You can imitate this ritual with a "nose hug." Simply cup your
hand gently over the dog's muzzle and give a little squeeze. The
warm and gentle pressure of your hand over the muzzle gives the
same message as the muzzle being gently mouthed. And you don't
get hair between your teeth doing it.

How does a subordinate wolf respond to a muzzle mouthing?
He answers by licking the alpha wolf under the chin. Most dogs
simply wag their tails. If you have used a nose hug because your
dog was acting wild, it should help calm him down.

I have read many dog books that advise people to pet their dogs
under the chin. Because all dogs speak wolf, it is not a terrific idea
to stroke a dog where a subordinate would lick. This is not a

Who's a good boy?

Dexter is! A nose hug gives a dog a delicious sense of security.

message I wish to give any dog. I have even heard of people getting bitten immediately after petting a dog under the chin. I prefer to scratch a dog behind his ears or reach around and scratch his chest, making him feel good without telling him something that could be dangerous.

9. Give Your Dog Appropriate Room and Board

Your dog is a pack animal and company is good for him. Unless there's a reason not to, I always advise people to let their dogs sleep in their bedrooms. I do not, however, advise letting the dog sleep on the bed. This does not mean you can't invite your dog onto the bed in the morning for kisses or call him up to keep you company when you have the flu. But actually sharing sleeping space makes the dog feel instantly equal and a moment later, superior (remember Dog Law 3). Dogs on the bed tend to get bossy and aggressive. They start by hogging the bed, move quickly on to growling if you roll over during the night and in no time they carry their aggression off the bed, out of the bedroom and into the rest of your relationship.

Every dog owner with a problem dog hopes for a miracle cure, the magic pill. Here's one I actually participated in.

I got a call from a neighbor with a Westie and a bad problem. Alan is crazy about his dog and they have always gotten along very well. Then recently, Billy began to growl at Alan if Alan moved at all in bed. Soon afterward Billy would growl when Alan tried to put his harness on him. That's when Alan became afraid.

He asked if I'd work with him and I promised I would. "But until we get together," I said, "keep Billy off the bed." Since Alan and Billy live in a studio apartment, we decided he should let Billy sleep in his dog bed, gated in the kitchen. Two days later Alan called to say that the problem was solved. Billy was sleeping happily in the kitchen and he was back to his old sweet self. I see Alan and Billy out walking everyday, best buddies once more.

Before you count on a miracle yourself, this is my only magic pill in more than twenty years of training dogs.

The message is, if you have a problem with your dog, keep him off the bed. If you don't want to start having a problem with your dog, give him a bed of his own and let him use it. Having your dog in your bedroom is a plus, usually for dog and owner. More than that is risky. Dogs too easily get the idea that they can run things and sleeping on the bed can make even a fairly mild dog possessive and bratty.

Some adolescent dogs eat like they are on steroids, while others suffer from fluctuating appetites. When your adolescent dog leaves his food, simply pitch it or refrigerate it, offering it again at the next meal. If you sweeten the pot, adding little goodies to get him to eat, you'll become a slave in no time. Skipping a meal now and again will not harm your dog; it will only spark his erratic appetite.

10. Teach Your Dog Some Limits

In order for your dog to grow up to be friendly and well-mannered, you have to monitor his behavior and teach him what he can do and can't do. This should be pretty obvious—he can chew his bone, he can't chew your couch; he can relieve himself in the yard, he can't do it indoors; he can eat at his bowl in the kitchen, he can't cruise the dining room table. These are the things you may have been teaching him since he was a little tyke. But there's more to monitor when your dog gets to be a teen.

The biggest mistake owners make is in not monitoring a dog's protectiveness—barking at the door, barking at strangers, acting aggressive toward people you let into your home or people you pass in the street. Some people are afraid that if they try to curb their dog's protective instinct, he won't protect them if they need it. As a result, the dog feels he's in charge of safety. Without monitoring, your dog's hit list grows and grows. You may even find yourself on it one day.

People want more than is reasonable from their dogs. Do you want a dog who is great with your kids, won't bite them or their friends, is fabulous with you but would lay down his life to protect your family, your house and all your possessions? So sorry. This dog doesn't exist.

The dog who is allowed to feel he is in charge of protection is like a loaded gun in the hands of a kid. If he is not monitored, he will "protect" you right into a lawsuit, making even your children's friends into his "enemies." You cannot allow your dog to be in charge. When he barks at the door because someone is knocking, thank him by saying, "Good dog," and then shut him up and off with, "Enough!" Don't let him block the doorway. Put him on a sit–stay, out of the way. Don't let him be like Roger was, lungeing at people in the street. It's rude, dangerous and highly inappropriate. He will be more likely to bite you than protect you if this continues. The adolescent dog's confidence keeps building until he is one and a half to three years old, depending on the breed and individual. So if you have a hair-trigger nine-month-old, just imagine what he'll be like in a year. Adolescence is the time to tell your dog that you make the decisions and you are in charge.

11. Be a Caretaker

Part of being in charge means that you are responsible for your dog's care and health. He doesn't like going to the veterinarian for shots? Too bad. Like it or not, he needs proper inoculations and medical attention. He also needs to be clean and groomed. He needs his coat brushed out and kept free of snarls. He needs to have his ears and teeth cleaned. Yes, his teeth. You can—and should—buy him a special toothbrush and toothpaste made just for dogs. He also needs his nails trimmed regularly to keep his feet healthy and his gait proper. If you don't or can't do all of these things, it may indicate a problem in the relationship. If your dog

Like it or not, he has to go for a checkup and shots.

sees you as his leader, if he properly respects you, he will, even if it's reluctantly, let you clean his ears, give him a bath and, most difficult, cut his nails. As his caretaker, your job is to insist on it.

12. Teach Your Dog Some Games

So that winning your dog's respect doesn't make you feel like an ogre, start your game playing now, even before your problems are solved. In this way, you can gradually replace negative behavior with fun, fun that *you* design and *you* direct. You should be the one to make up the rules for the game. You should be the one to initiate the game. Honey, that's alpha.

As your dog's problems get solved and he becomes more fun and less of a headache, he, too, can initiate games. He can even win—as long as you play with him the way his mother would have.

WINNING AND LOSING

Years ago I had a client who used to drive me crazy by letting his Doberman occasionally ignore the very commands I was working so hard to get him to obey. "He has to win sometimes," he told me, and he wouldn't listen when I told him he had picked the wrong place for the dog to win.

MOTHER KNOWS BEST

When a mother dog plays with her puppies, she lets the puppies *play* at alpha. It is part of their early education to practice at being grown-up dogs, to try on grown-up roles, much in the way you or I played dress-up with daddy's hat or mommy's high heels.

The bitch will roll over on her back, taking on the submissive posture of a low-ranked pack member and let the puppies charge her, leap on her, tug at her, win. When the lesson is over, when mother has had enough sharp little teeth grabbing at her sensitive ears and tail, she will turn back over, give the puppies one slam with her foreleg and walk off.

Mother knows that when educational games are over, she must remind the rest of the pack, yet again, that she is in charge. This she does with graceful efficiency. Play is fun, but it also teaches her puppies what they need to learn in order to survive. Given that fact, it would be poor mothering to end a game without a neat little reminder of reality. After all, puppies' memories are short.

It would also be poor mothering to let the puppies "win" *at all* when safety was the issue. When a puppy strays beyond its mother's circle of safety, it will be corrected quickly, firmly and with no games played. Mother knows clearly when fun and games are the appropriate fare for puppies and when they are not.

When we take over the role of top dog, the mother's role, if you will, we, too, must distinguish between matters of life and limb and matters of game playing. Obedience training is the surest tool an owner has for ensuring the safety of his dog. To play games and let the dog "win" after a command is issued is to guarantee poor obedience from your pet. A speedy recall or drop from a distance can not only save a dog's life, it often has. But a dog's mind cannot embrace the threat of traffic and he must not be allowed to think he can "win" when it could cost him his life.

Like the mother dog, you *can* let your dog win when you play games. It will help you raise a lively, happy, confident, well-exercised animal.

Scarlet, my German Shepherd, likes to win so much, she cheats. When we play our game of running bases, tearing through the house like idiots, eyes ablaze, feet skidding on the wooden floors, Scarlet will sometimes double back to the base we just left in order to prove conclusively who the more clever of us truly is. Even playing it straight, she's surely fast enough to win. But she enjoys the extra points she gains by "fooling" me and the fantastic sparkle in her eyes when she has cheated and I arrive, out of breath and late, at the base of *her* choice, lets me know for sure that what she did was no accident. I like to let Scarlet win when we play games, even when she cheats. It's good for her. But as a responsible top dog, I take my cue from the mother dog. When I am too out of breath from running and laughing to continue the game, I always make sure *I* win the final round. I don't even mind cheating to do so.

WORK VS PLAY

Dogs can distinguish between work and play. They will glee-fully accept the chance to play at alpha, whether they are still young enough to be with their mothers or are ten years old, like my Shepherd "puppy." But if your messages are mixed, if you let them win at work, or if you don't win at the end of a play session, the serious side of your training program gets lost. Mixed mes-sages make for a mixed-up relationship.

When teaching your dog, and keep in mind that these clever students are learning truths even when we think we're just fooling around, always consider how a situation appears *to the dog*. For example, one day Scarlet and I were walking past a woman and her dog who were sitting on the stoop of a town house. When the dog saw Scarlet, he stood up and barked aggressively. The woman told him "No," but at the same time, she began to tap or pat him on his side. Clearly *she* thought she was correcting her dog for inappropriate aggression. Clearly *he* thought he was being praised. This sort of mixed message is quite common. Many people pet their dogs to "calm" them when the dog is inappropriately noisy or aggressive, when the dog is acting out his fear by bolting or hiding, when the dog is carrying on in an obnoxious way to gain attention. The lips say no, no, but the message of that tap, tap, tap, is viewed by the dog as positive reenforcement. When there is a mixed message, a yes and a no, the dog is free to pick and choose.

My client's Doberman always worked for me. Sam had had a successful show career and was bored silly hanging around the house or kennel. I felt that the best way to teach him was to establish a routine that he could look forward to. Sam lived in the suburbs, so I drove him to the center of town in order to be able to work with distractions around. Sam was a big show-off and not only got my attention for working well, but that of everyone who saw him. Sam loved an audience and learned very quickly in this atmosphere. Next, we'd go to a quiet side street for Sam's favorite game, one I made up just for him. But we would only play Sam's game, a game in which he was the winner, when he had given me what I was after in the training lesson. Sam comprehended the deal fully and only once did he act so stubborn that I was forced to skip the game. At the end of the game, during which I pretended that Sam was too strong for me and let him pull me stumbling along down the block, I would quickly run through all the commands, offering lavish praise, thus reestablishing myself as alpha in the traditional way that all dogs understand. And last, back at the kennel, I'd brush Sam's smooth, black coat and whisper sweet nonsense in his ear. Affection was clearly part of the message I wanted to leave with Sam.

So lighten up your training program with wonderful, dog-centered games, but be sure that the message the dog gleans from his contact with you is not one that will do him—or your training program—harm. His safety depends upon this.

GAMES TO PLAY

Begin with something as easy as a game of catch. Put your dog on a sit-stay. Tell your dog, "Catch it!" and toss a small bite of dog biscuit right at his mouth. Unless he knows how to catch already, he'll probably let the first ten pieces bounce off his face. Not to worry. He'll catch on. Just let him break (after you say Okay) and eat the pieces he missed. After a day or two, he'll begin to open his mouth and try to catch the bait. Now you can increase his motivation to succeed by only letting him eat what he catches.

Once your dog gets pretty good at catching, he'll start to like the game for itself, not just for the food. This is the time to switch to a ball. Take his favorite, tell him, "Catch it!" and toss it at his mouth. When he misses, just get the ball and try again. When he catches the ball, go nuts. Applaud for him. Hoot for him. Tell him he's the greatest dog that was ever born.

Raise your expectations once again. This time, after he catches the ball, call him to come. Say, "Hold it!" as he approaches and then tell him, "Out!" to get him to drop the ball into your hand. If your fun-loving teen plays keep away with his retrieved treasure, play with his leash attached. Now when you call him to come, if he dances sideways, cheerfully and gently reel him in. Don't get angry. Remember, even though you and your dog are both learning from each other, this is still a game. So keep it fun.

Getting your dog to hold the ball, come to you and deliver it to your hand will take some practice, but it's worth the effort. It will make the game more complex and more fun. It will also help reenforce your role as top dog.

13. Teach a Trick with a Message

If you have not yet taught give your paw to your dog, now is the time to do so. The pawing gesture is a submissive gesture, so this easy, cute trick also reenforces your position, and that of any other person, as alpha. You can teach your dog to give his paw initially by pawing at him. If that doesn't get the response you want, hold out your hand, say "Give your paw," and pull his collar sideways, just an inch or two. The paw opposite the direction you are pulling will come up for balance. Grasp it, shake it and praise like crazy.

Once your dog begins to give his paw, he can practice with everyone. After all, the message underneath the trick is valid—he should be subordinate to all people. This trick becomes a kind of coded reminder of his position as a beloved pet.

Some trainers have written that give your paw is an exercise to humiliate dogs by making them act submissive. This saddens me greatly. Perhaps these trainers need to visit their local shelters to understand how urgently important it is that people raise their dogs to feel and exhibit gentle, submissive behavior. When your adolescent dog slaps his big, fat paw into your hand and you kiss and pet and praise him, he will feel anything but humiliated.

WHERE
YOU BELONG

As you work on convincing yourself and your adolescent dog that you are the natural and rightful leader of this person–dog pack, don't forget why you wanted a dog in the first place. Whatever problems you may have to work out, he's still your companion, your friend. He's funny, full of energy and playful. He's got a zest for living that's endless, and contagious. Despite his overblown ego, he's a great dog, your pal. As you learn how to win your dog's respect and as you move to the place where you belong, alpha, your bond with the dog will markedly increase. The less time you spend cleaning up accidents, chasing a dog who won't come, correcting broken commands and putting up with the bratty behavior of a dog who's too full of himself, the more time you'll have for all the good things having a dog is all about.

4
TOOLS OF
THE TRADE

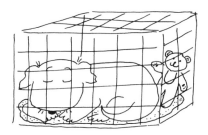

Ilive in a dog-loving neighborhood, so when I look out my office windows, I almost always see people walking their dogs. I enjoy watching without being seen because when people don't know they are being observed, they talk to their dogs and relate to them in the most charming ways. Even the person who seems lost in thought, all but ignoring the family member on the other end of the leash, reveals the relationship via body language. There is a loving patience that shows up in the human as the dog sniffs his way around the territory. Sometimes there is a lack of same and a dog in the middle of an urgent performance may get pulled along, ready or not. Of course, it's at least as revealing to observe the scene the other way around, starting with the dog and trying to see the relationship as revealed in his attitude. Show me a dog ignoring the human he has in tow and I'll show you a relationship in need of repair.

I can understand the person who is preoccupied while his dog relieves himself and gets a little exercise. We humans have a lot on our minds and lots of responsibilities. But a dog's only responsibility is to pay attention to his master. So the dog who takes his daily constitutional as if he were alone or as if his beloved owner were some annoying weight at the end of the leash should be taught to think otherwise, for his own safety if for no other reason. There are several reasons why this happens. First and foremost, the relationship is off. There's heavy confusion as to who's in charge. Second, the level of training is poor. A trained dog knows for sure who has what role. Third, the owner may be using a flexible or extendable leash. The dog hits the street and then hits the end of the leash. Now he's twenty, twenty-five feet ahead of his owner and couldn't care less about the poor sap who feeds him, walks him, pays all his bills. The street is the *last* place you want your dog to forget your existence. What if you should drop the leash or he should slip out of his collar? In addition, you cannot train or make a proper correction with an extendable leash. The "leash" part is very unfriendly to the human hand.

Of course, a proper walk for a dog does *not* mean that he's working all the time or simply staring up at his owner's face with no other thought in his head. When Dexter hits the street, it's playtime. He lives to meet and greet, to play joyfully with other dogs and to smooch every willing person he meets. This is just fine with me. But when I walk him, I use not a twelve- or fifteen-foot leash but a four- or a six-foot leash. I want him nearby, even when he's on a free walk and not heeling. When we walk on quiet streets and no potential playmates are in sight, I will occasionally say his name, "Dex-ter," very softly. He turns, he smiles, he comes back to me. I pet him and he goes right back to his free walk. Even when we meet another friendly dog, eventually the other owner or I will have to continue on. A dog must learn to keep a tiny bit of his consciousness reserved for you, even when he's playing. In fact, by doing so, by remembering that you are his alpha, he is more likely to get along with the other dogs he meets. After all, because of you, he's secure. You have signaled to him that he may socialize and play. He has no reason to start a fight.

When people come to me with problems, we walk around outside with the dog. If I see that the dog is ignoring his owner, I ask the owner simply to stop walking, thus effectively stopping the dog from walking—at least after he gets to the end of his leash. Then we wait for the dog to turn around. For the rare dog who won't turn and look even when you stop, simply crouch and whistle or call his name. With either method, initially the dog may turn and look annoyed, as if to say, "What happened? Did your feet fall off?" Praise him for looking and continue your walk. As time goes on, this little game starts to change. The dog, because he is praised for turning to check where you are, does it more easily and in a better mood. Soon enough, when you stop, he'll turn and come right to you, eyes all crinkly, tail wagging. In response, love him up and send him along. Teaching your dog to remember you exist is just that easy. I usually do two "stops" on a long walk. I don't like to badger my dogs. Understanding that training is a long-term process gives me the patience to work slowly. Going slowly is the way to go. It allows for *real* change to take place.

The first tool you need for reshaping your adolescent dog is a good leather leash. Traditionally, obedience training called for a six-foot leash. If you have one, you can always keep part of it looped if you want your dog closer to you. Sometimes I prefer a four-foot leash. It still gives Dexter room to play and when he's walking free he's not too far from me. Cotton web leashes are okay. You can fold them up and stuff them in your pocket when you get to the park. Nylon tends to burn when your dog pulls and most adolescent dogs forget themselves and pull sometimes. Chain leashes give me the willies. Not only do they hurt your hand if you grab them to make a correction, they can also snap and break if your dog suddenly lunges. Leather is by far the best choice. It is easiest on the hands and if you keep it out of your dog's mouth, it will last for years.

Never let your dog chew or tug on his leash when you walk or train him. A chewed leash demeans your authority. A chewed-up leash is highly dangerous. The first scenario may mean poor training and twelve bucks out the window. The second could mean a dead dog. When you get home, hang the leash on a hook inside your hall closet where you'll always be able to find it and your dog won't.

To what should you attach your new leather leash? For training all but the smallest dogs, I use a nylon slip collar. I find that the nylon collar, slipped up behind the ears when you are training, allows great control with the tiniest of corrections. Even on Dexter, who has a neck like Arnold Schwarzenegger, the nylon collar does the trick.

In addition to a training collar, every dog should have a flat or rolled buckle collar. I like leather because it softens with age and looks wonderful on just about every dog. If your dog spends his days swimming or rolling around in the mud, you might prefer nylon to leather. Nylon collars are reasonably priced, attractive and washable.

Using the right equipment will make raising and training your dog much easier. Most of what you need—a leather leash, a slip collar, a buckle collar, a few nearly indestructible toys, some sterilized bones, a few balls to chase and catch and a couple of stainless-steel pans for food and water—is not terribly expensive. The only costly item you'll need is a dog crate. But no matter the cost, I wouldn't dream of raising a dog without one.

The dog crate, a folding, wire cage with a solid tray on the bottom, becomes your dog's den. Every dog needs a room of his

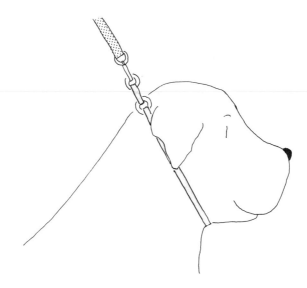

A nylon collar, slipped up behind the ears, allows for great control with the tiniest of corrections.

own, a place to retreat to when the world is too much for him, a place to be left safely when he is going through a destructive chewing period and can't be watched, a place in which to calm down when he gets the crazies, a place to sleep, in your room but off your bed, that smells and feels just right.

If your dog has never used a crate, take your time to introduce one to him. Open the crate, put it in a corner of your bedroom and put your dog's mat or pillow in the crate. Now put in a favorite toy and next place a favorite tidbit in the crate. If your dog just reaches in for the treat, praise him, try it once more and quit for the day.

Your dog may simply go into the crate to sleep, which would be easy and wonderful. After all, his pillow is in there. But what if he doesn't go in? Begin to feed your dog in his open crate. Place his food dish at the back of the crate, tell him "Okay" and walk away. If he wants to eat, he knows where his food is. Do not, at this time, close the door of the crate.

Working creatively and slowly, see if you can get your adolescent dog used to the crate. Once he uses it on his own or at least eats in the crate, you may begin to send him into the crate on command. Tell him, "Crate!" and tap inside the crate. If need be,

Every dog needs a room of her own.

toss in a treat. Once he's in, close the door, count three chimpan-zees and open the crate to let him out, clapping, hooting and praising. Try a second go, and quit for the day.

By working slowly, with praise and, if necessary, treats, your dog should become accustomed to his crate in a few weeks. Be sure to let him use it for at least an hour when you're home so he will be ready for it when you go out. At night, encourage your dog to stay off the bed and sleep in his crate in your room. If he goes into the crate on his own, let him be. It is his sanctuary and while in it, he should not be disturbed. So if he surpasses himself in rottenness one day and as you begin to rant and roll your eyes he runs to his crate, do not follow him. Know that you've done a good job of crate training and now the crate is yours to use when you are desperate and need it.

When should you use the crate with a half-grown dog? Certainly not all day long. The crate is excellent for keeping a dog safely contained, after exercise and a chance to relieve himself, for a period of two to three hours. If your dog is destructive when you aren't home, crate him while you are away. If his housebreaking slips and slides, use the crate and a schedule to get him back in tow. And when you have walked him, fed him, trained him and played with him and he still wants more, give him and yourself a twenty-minute "time-out" by putting your dog in his crate and leaving the room.

If your dog's behavior was caused by being too wired up and overtired, he will hit the crate, hit his pillow and be out before you leave the room. In any case, whether he sleeps or spends his crate time quietly gnawing on a bone, the enforced time-out will help you cope with his zaniness when you let him out.

The crate is great for any short-term need—keeping him safe when you are too busy to monitor him. But aside from its use as a permanent room with a view for your dog, door open at all times, its use as a tool should be limited. Used sparingly and thoughtfully, it can save your sanity. Overused, it can break the spirit of a good dog.

What if you need lots of time-outs because your dog is driving you nuts? You don't want to overuse the crate, but luckily there are alternatives. You can keep the dog in the room with you on a long down. You may have to get up to correct him the first few times you try this, but soon enough, you won't. Adolescent dogs

Tiring an adolescent with outdoor exercise is good!

have poor self-control, even when they know what's expected of them—and often they don't know, so the long down as outside control and a kind of time-out is great during meals. It teaches the dog to stay in the room with the family without begging and pestering. After a while, staying near the dinner table and just relaxing becomes a good habit.

The best time-out of all for teenage dogs is a play date. You can take your dog to the park where other owners bring their dogs to play and let him socialize, play, run around and get exhausted. The rest of your day will be easy and wonderful. A tired adolescent dog is like a gift from heaven! We also do in-house play dates. Dexter and his best friend, Jake, a Bernese Mountain Dog, visit each other at home. An hour of indoor play can also result in wonderfully mellow, tired dogs. If you live in the suburbs, your dog and his guest may be able to play in the basement or, even better, in your fenced yard. Not having those choices in New York City, we do the unthinkable and let our dog and his pals play in the living room.

Tiring an adolescent dog with a play period, outdoor exercise or a good, half-hour-long obedience lesson will give you the peace and quiet you crave while he sleeps and gets ready to be cheerful and full of beans all over again.

While your tired teen sleeps, you can enjoy the peace and quiet you crave.

TOYS FOR
YOUR TEEN

Most adolescent dogs favor and play with a certain toy for several weeks and then one day demolish it. Do the best you can in choosing durable playthings, but remember that dog toys are not meant to last forever. Certain toys, like balls or Frisbees, can be put away when you are not using them with your dog. In this way, they will not only remain intact, they will also remain special to your dog.

What about chew things? Dogs do not outgrow the need to chew. Chewing can help relieve your dog's anxiety when he is left alone, and even when you're home, he can have hours of pleasure chewing on rawhide or on a sterilized bone. Ask your veterinarian which type of chew things he recommends for your dog.

You can save a lot of money when you shop for equipment for your dog by crossing the following items off your list.

No matter how big and tough your dog is, you won't need a

spike or prong collar. The nylon slip collar, moved up behind the dog's ears, gives you all the control you need.

You cannot obedience train a dog using a harness, so unless you have a Malamute and a sled, or a dog with a trachea problem, you won't need one. (Trachea problems occur mostly in toy breeds such as the Yorkshire Terrier, Chihuahua, Pomeranian and Toy Poodle. A dog suffering from collapsed trachea syndrome will have a dry, honking cough. A properly used slip collar cannot cause this condition, but it could exacerbate the condition in a dog that is already suffering from the syndrome. If you have a toy breed that honks like a goose, see your veterinarian and do not use a slip collar. I never use slip collars on small dogs anyway. Most will work beautifully on a buckle collar.)

You won't need a can full of pennies to throw at your dog. It's just a silly way to make a correction. When your dog respects you properly, you can simply "throw" your voice at him, by saying "no," "down" or "off," as the occasion requires.

You won't need a head halter for your adolescent dog unless you're pregnant or have a condition or injury that impairs your balance. The head halter restrains your dog; he just won't pull with his face the way he would with his neck. But when you use the head halter, your dog will not be getting trained. The moment you take it off, he'll be his same old pulling self. Still, if *while* you are in the process of training him and before he becomes reliable you need this piece of equipment to prevent yourself from getting pulled down and injured, it is available and worth using. For the long term, I prefer a slip collar and obedience training.

Throw your voice, not a can full of pennies.

What about the shock collar, now so widely advertised? Would this be a suitable way to get the job of training done quickly, a shortcut worth considering?

I have worked with dogs who have become phobic or aggressive after the use of shock collars or "invisible" fences. The use of electricity seems, in some cases, to cause a phobia that goes underground, surfacing as a fear of children, cars, other dogs, elevators, anything. The dog may show no emotion about the collar or the "fence," but months later act crazy or bite "for no reason." To me, having a dog means having a great relationship, a friend. And using a shock collar is just not something you'd do to a friend. Save your money! More important, save your dog!

Last of all, you can save money on treats. Of course, your dog can have snacks. But you won't need them for training. They only show a dog how insecure you feel. Instead, we'll work on your knowledge, skill and confidence. Those last longer and they're free. Even more important, the self-esteem you gain succeeding with your dog's training program will spill over into the rest of your life, and amen to that.

Remember yourself as an adolescent!

You will need time, patience, a sense of humor and a commitment to see the job of educating your dog through. You won't need guilt, yet I see it in a lot of my retrains. Look at it this way. Suppose you have made some mistakes in raising your dog. You may have been given poor advice, or you may have made a decision without enough information. Perhaps you just got so frustrated you didn't know what was right anymore. This does not make you a bad person. In fact, the energy you spend feeling guilty that you didn't do everything perfectly with your puppy in the first place is energy unavailable for working and playing with your dog now. It doesn't help him and it makes you feel awful. So as of right now, let's assume the slate is clean. You've got a dog you love, and you're getting your act together. Your dog would probably be a bratty adolescent no matter what you did when he was a puppy. (Remember yourself as an adolescent!) Now you're getting the equipment you need and you're going to get your energetic adolescent out and exercise him, play with him, train him up. But first, let's look at the way professional trainers work, how they get more mileage out of the time they put in as well as the way they respond to the different character types dogs display.

Part
Two

"A trained dog willingly does what its owner asks."

THE MERCK VETERINARY MANUAL, 7TH EDITION

5

IS YOUR DOG
A CHARACTER?

Before I became a professional dog trainer, I did my dog's daily practice sessions for a variety of reasons. I practiced with my dog because I wanted him to be trained. I was proud of him when he learned something new. I practiced because, usually, I enjoyed working with my dog. Most of all, I practiced with my dog because I was afraid of making an idiot of myself in class the following week. I was afraid of humiliation, scorn, guffawing from my peers, sarcasm from my teacher. Lastly, I practiced because I was compulsive, obedient and, let's face it, a wimp. I did as I was told—to the letter. I didn't add anything. I didn't do anything differently from the way it had been done in class.

When I became a professional trainer, my practice sessions changed. Because I was now working with other people's dogs, and because I was earning my living by training dogs, I had to work more efficiently. I had to be prepared, too, for a great variety of responses. That meant that I had to have a greater variety of tricks up my sleeve in order to get the job done. Once I became a professional dog trainer, I always worked with a plan—my own. I always had both short- and long-term goals in mind. I always let each dog's behavior fire my mind to come up with new, creative solutions to old problems. I always kept notes—and still do, even with my own pet dogs. And I always took into account the breed of the dog, what he was bred to do, how that work function affected his behavior or helped create his problems, how it determined his likes and dislikes, his energy level, his obsessions. I researched each breed, reading and rereading the breed standards.

I studied canine character types, too. It helps to know if the dog you are training is independent or takes direction well, if he's stubborn or easygoing, if he's lethargic and slow to move or quicksilver in his reactions. It is good practice to look at each dog as an individual and figure out his particular character traits apart from what the breed standard promises because not every purebred dog conforms to his breed standard, nor does every dog have a breed or a standard to which you can refer. A great many of the dogs I have trained are randomly bred dogs, yet each has and reveals his own individual and interesting style. Knowing a dog's character can help you educate him better and appreciate and enjoy him all the more.

Before and after each lesson, I thought about the dog and how he worked—or didn't work. This way, I was faster, more efficient, and more successful in reaching my goal, a trained dog. I even liked the work better, because when you're good at something, you enjoy doing it.

Can you use a professional trainer's secret methods to elevate the level of your training, to be happier as you work, to become more efficient, faster, more successful in reaching your goal, a trained dog? You bet you can!

HOW SMART
IS YOUR DOG?

All dogs are different. Each one, though somewhat predictable through knowledge of his species and breed, is an individual to be studied, understood and educated according to his own intelligence, tractability and interesting quirks. When in an obedience training class with your dog, compare him to the Sheltie next to you only for educational purposes. If you deem him dumber because he does not learn as quickly or as well, you may be mistaken. Though he *may* be dumber, more likely he's simply another type of dog, more stubborn, independent or aloof. Because of his breeding (and don't forget that every mixed breed dog carries genetic input as well) he may *need* to work on his own, work far from his handler, think for himself. These traits, though they may occasionally frustrate you when you want instant, cheerful obedience, are admirable qualities. The independent dog, creative thinker or problem solver can be an unendingly interesting companion.

Motivation plays a big part in a dog's desire to use his natural intelligence. When my Golden Retriever bitch, Fanny, was in heat, my male Golden, Oliver, was sent out to the backyard to cool his jets. Unable to manipulate me into opening the back door, even with pitiful whining and that sad look in his big, brown eyes, he jumped the fence that separated the backyard from the front yard, came to the front door, stood on his hind legs and rang the doorbell. I was so impressed with the cleverness of his spectacular trick that I included it in *Dog Tricks, Teaching Your Dog To Be Useful, Fun and Entertaining*, a book I co-authored with Captain Arthur Haggerty.

Motivation is the key to training your adolescent dog. A proper relationship—you're alpha, he isn't—and your can-do attitude will do wonders for what now may seem like a challenged learner.

Most people judge a dog's intelligence by his trainability, but this alone does not reveal a dog's IQ. How should intelligence be judged in a dog anyway? The Beagle, who takes forever to housebreak and obedience train, might very well put a more trainable dog to shame on a rabbit hunt. So if, like me, you are a pet owner and do not use your dog in the way his genetic program-

He can roust a rodent from its nest.

ming designed him to be employed, do not blame him for excelling in an area you care nothing about and not doing as well in something you do. Appreciate and work with what you have. Instead of thinking, "Why didn't you get it right like that Sheltie!" you'll be pleased with the progress your dog makes when you compare him to no one other than himself.

In order to plan the perfect training program for your teen, it helps to know what type of dog he is. If he is a purebred, your job will surely be easier. First, read and reread the standard for his breed. Be aware of the work he was bred to do, for that is the key to his type or personality. The Fox Terrier, bred to go to ground and roust a rodent from its nest, does not have a feisty, never-say-die attitude for nothing. The difficult-to-housebreak Beagle was designed to work in a pack, so he was selected for his ability to get along with others. The ability to keep clean or not keep clean indoors was not a factor since packs were not housed indoors. Studying the breed history can tell you a lot about how your breed should think and react because when it comes to dogs, what you see is *not* what you get. You get infinitely more than meets the eye. Along with every pretty face, that with which we fall in love, there's a complete set of talents and instincts which were honed

He was selected for his ability to get along with others.

and strengthened for generations. Maybe you can ignore or forget this fact. But your dog simply cannot. His talents, instincts and predispositions are built in and no training in the world is going to remove them.

FUNCTION
SHAPES THE DOG

Suppose you fall in love with a nice, big Labrador Retriever. He's so much more than beautiful to behold and good with kids. He was bred to work and, even without knowing the text of his standard, becomes electrified at the sight of a duck. Yet, as dogs go, he's easy. Give him a good amount of exercise and the chance to retrieve, preferably from water, and he'll be a happy dog. He does not have to schlep dead ducks to feel fulfilled.

A herding dog may not be so easy. An Old English Sheepdog will view your family as having great flock potential. Every herding dog worth his chow will take responsibility for his family's safety, particularly that of the children. Is it his fault that it's easier to keep an eye on everyone after he herds them into a tight little group? Is it his fault that generations of genes make it automatic for him to circle and nip in order to keep his flock small and safe?

This, after all, is who he is. This dog needs more than exercise and training. He needs to be prevented from herding when children are his flock.

How about that Malamute, the one with the big "S" on his chest. Here, for generations, breeders selected for strength, independence and courage. No way would his kind get that sled to the Pole if he looked back to you for approval every ten seconds. He moves to the beat of a different drummer. He's his own dog, not yours. Ask not why he looks you in the eye and yanks the leash from your hand. He does it because he can. He's not a dog to be acquired thoughtlessly, yet many do.

The natty cuteness of the terrier is only part of the picture. His who–elected–you–president? attitude was not put there to frustrate your desire to have an obedient dog. His scrappy nature, his marine-yell barking, his if-this-way-doesn't-work-there-are-twenty-other-routes view of the world are all necessary for the job he was bred to do. Rodent extermination is not a task for wimps. His character and ability do not disappear when he becomes a pet.

The burning need to run, the obsession with collecting animals or humans into a manageable grouping, the passion for carrying feathered things to alpha, the ability to haul, point, flush, guard or run between the wheels of a coach, all the things that once upon a time were necessary work functions, are still within our dogs. And if, like me, you are awed and moved by what dogs were bred to do, you take their functions seriously. You try to find an appropriate way your dogs can express their talents. You are also aware of how and when these instincts can present a problem.

Understanding your dog's work function can change your frustration into admiration. What a dog *can* do is far more important than the fact that he may take longer to learn a sit-stay than the Collie next door. Discovering *who* you are training will not only be an interesting journey, it will also make it easier to teach that sit-stay with appropriate expectations. This is *not* an invitation to make excuses for your dog and give up. Far from it! It is, instead, an invitation to have realistic expectations. You probably will not get your Siberian Husky off-leash trained. Spitz breeds are runners. If you take them out into the wide open spaces and take off the leash, they take off. And, yes, Boxers are stubborn, Dalmatians need lots of exercise, German Shepherds are highly trainable, but *still* too strong for many people, Finnish Spitz tend to be noisy, and it does indeed take longer to house train a hound than it does a Poodle. But so what? Within reason, all dogs can be trained well enough to be well-mannered, enjoyable pets. By understanding breed and type differences, you can avoid a really bad case of gene blues when your little puppy grows to adolescence and shows what he's made of. After all, the energetic adolescent can be a formidable malcontent when he's untrained, underexercised and, God help us all, unemployed. How sad this is! Once you learn about your dog's work abilities, you will understand which can be rerouted into obedience work, tracking, field work, pet-assisted therapy or jogging, and which you should be cautious about, instincts such as herding, which, when they are not used as originally planned, can be a nuisance or a danger.

A long, happy relationship with a dog is based on meatier stuff than initial attraction. But even if you fell in love with a pretty face and took home a puppy you didn't know much about, once you understand the whole dog, what he'll be like as a companion, what his needs are, where potential trouble lies and how to avoid it, you will be able to plan a workable, appropriate program for the two of you to follow.

Even if you have a mixed-breed dog, you may be able to study his body type and make an educated guess about what group he loosely falls into. Our pup, Dexter, looks like some kind of bull and terrier mix. More important, he acts like a bull and terrier dog. He has all the isn't-it-simply-grand-to-be-alive cheerfulness of a terrier, even before his first cup of morning coffee. He also has exactly the you-and-who-else bulldog stubbornness his muscular body and powerful, low-slung physique would let you believe he'd have. Not expecting him to learn like something he isn't is helping me to train him appropriately.

So, if not by the breed or look of your dog then by what he reveals of his personality and character type, you will find out who you have on the other end of your leash and be able to use that information to help you educate your dog. In some cases, ours for example, knowing the dog is a stubborn type helps me to be patient and prevents me from feeling like a failure. Had I compared Dexter to the Border Collie in his obedience class, expecting him to be as obedient, willing to please and disgustingly perfect as she was, I would have slit my wrists.

It is important to note that your dog will not simply be *one* of the following character types, any more than you would be. My clients Sheila and Howie talk of their dog Blue's "good days and bad days." On her good days, Blue is friendly, fairly obedient, pretty tractable. On her bad days, Blue is stubborn, spooky, difficult to manage. Most dogs, like most humans, have good days and bad days. This will be especially so during your dog's adolescence. Adolescence exaggerates whatever characteristics a dog has. Most dogs also have many-faceted characters. Adolescence helps differentiate the many aspects of a dog's personality.

These thumbnail sketches are not meant to pigeonhole your dog, but instead to give you some added hints of how to understand and think about your dog and the work you are doing with him.

First we'll look at character distinctions as they tend to run in families, terriers vs herding dogs vs sight hounds, etc. These descriptions of family groupings include a wide range of breeds and of necessity will be very general. They are not meant to accurately describe any given breed or any particular dog. They are only meant to give you a starting point, an idea of the broad type of dog you will find in a particular group—for example, if your dog's relatives were bred to work closely with man and thus have a strong desire to serve and please, or if their most powerful genetic input involved getting along with a group of their own kind and developing skills that would enable them to follow a trail and find game. After this glimpse at family groupings, we'll examine character traits, distinctions that can show up in any dog of any breed and in any combination with other traits.

CANINE
BREED TYPES

SPORTING DOGS This family includes Retrievers, Pointers, Spaniels, Setters, the Weimaraner, the Brittany, the Vizsla, etc.

The average sporting dog has been bred to work with man rather than on his own and so, with training, usually makes a tractable pet. However, some of the sporting dogs were bred to work at a distance and these dogs may go far from you when let off the leash. With obedience training, you can call them back. But you must understand that the dog's desire to roam or hunt faraway is built in.

Well-bred, well-socialized sporting dogs tend to be good with children and make wonderful pets. It is not difficult with most to replace the work they were bred to do with obedience work, tracking, games, swimming and fun retrieving.

Sporting dogs do need more exercise than most people realize. Naturally, the bigger the dog, the more space his exercise tends to require. These dogs are hunters and have the capacity to put in a full day's work. Left alone at home without sufficient exercise, many tend to be destructive.

Some sporting breeds have another sort of problem, one caused by the strong work function that was selectively bred for. Some of these dogs are so "birdy" that you will have trouble holding their attention when they are out of doors. Every scent distracts them and pulls their attention away from you. Begin your training indoors and only move outside when you have good attention from your dog inside. Even then, some of these dogs, particularly field stock, will try your patience. Remember not to blame the dog. He didn't choose his own parents.

In general, sporting breeds tend to be quite responsive to training and have a strong desire to please their owners. Expect a long adolescence with these dogs. They won't seem to mature until they are at least three years old.

WORKING DOGS   This family includes the Boxer, Rottweiler, Bernese Mountain Dog, Doberman Pinscher, St. Bernard, and Mastiff among others. The American Kennel Club includes the Siberian Husky, Samoyed and Alaskan Malamute in this group. For a better description of these sled dogs, see the Spitz group below.

Many of the working dogs are so intelligent it can be frightening and, as a result, they need an intelligent training program. They do not have the tolerance for repetition that the sporting dogs have and may quit working if they are really bored. Always work far ahead of your goals when training a working dog, adding games, different settings for practice sessions and variety in the order of commands to be practiced.

Working dogs can be more than pets. They can be true companions because of their brightness and attitude of service, but if you want your working dog to be really happy, he will need education, occupation and exercise on a regular basis.

All of the working breeds need to have their protective instincts monitored and to learn from their owner what is appropriate and what is not. The working breed that reaches adolescence without having been taught to suppress some of his protectiveness will be an obnoxious, even dangerous, teenager. Remember the formidable size and strength of some of these breeds and remember that adolescent dogs have poor judgment and even poorer self control. Control should always come from the master, not the dog.

TERRIERS The terrier group includes the Bull Terrier, Miniature Schnauzer, Airedale, Irish, Kerry Blue, Soft Coated Wheaten, Australian, Cairn, Border, Skye, Scottish, Smooth Fox Terrier and others with *terrier* in their name.

The terrier is the quintessential teenager for all his life. No matter how old your terrier is, you are reading the right book.

The terrier is an energetic, jolly, stubborn dog, ever ready to play, often with a chip on his shoulder when it comes to playing with other dogs. A terrier will learn quickly but hardly find time in his schedule to obey. He's ever busy, ever moving, ever full of fun and often full of the devil.

Training a terrier simply means you must be more stubborn than the terrier. Teaching through games will keep a terrier's attention far better than teaching by rote. Never give up. If you do, your terrier will know you did and be all the more difficult to teach next time you get desperate enough to try. Besides, your terrier *will* learn. Asta and Toto were terriers. President Franklin Roosevelt's Scottish Terrier, Fala, had manners good enough for the White House and presidential motorcades. With work, one day your terrier, too, can be more than a wildly fun pet; he can also be fairly obedient.

SPITZ DOGS This family includes the Alaskan Malamute, Samoyed, Siberian Husky, Akita, Shiba Inu, Finnish Spitz, Chow Chow, Pomeranian, etc. Spitz breeds are found all over the world. All have some form of the classic wedge-shaped head, small, thick, pointed, erect ears, a double coat and a tail which is carried curled over the back.

Spitz breeds are among the most beautiful, charming and manipulative creatures in the dog world. They just have a way of winding their owners and even total strangers around their pretty paws. Living with a member of the Spitz family is an unforgettable experience and will keep you on your toes.

Most Spitz breeds learn very quickly but have very little motivation to obey. They will do everything for you on a leash but if you take the leash off out of doors, you could get an ever-diminishing glimpse of the back end of your dog. Spitz dogs tend to run. It has nothing to do with their love for you or lack of it. They all seem to be trying to get to the North Pole as fast as possible!

Train your Spitz breed with patience and with a plan, accomplishing at each lesson exactly what you plan to, not what your gorgeous and adorable Spitz breed has planned for the lesson. For all the extra effort and herculean grooming these dogs require, the love and affection they give in return is extraordinary. You may curse them, but you'll probably go out and do it again.

SIGHT HOUNDS Ibizan, Basenji, Greyhound, Saluki, Whippet, Afghan, Pharaoh Hound, Borzoi, Irish Wolfhound, etc.

Sight hounds have a reputation for not being the brightest dogs around, in other words, just a pretty face. Indeed, these beauties are among the most gorgeous and graceful in dogdom, but they are not dumb. Here again work function determines the character of the dog. So these dogs always have both an ear and an eye out for game. They are, however, trainable dogs and usually can be trained with a very light touch. In other words, you should strive to reach your dog mentally rather than coercing him to work for you. These are not dogs to yank around, yell at or, heaven forbid, strike. They are sensitive animals that respond to kindness, clarity, humor and, above all, respect.

Sight hounds, who often hunted in packs, tend to get along well with other dogs and can work well with other dogs. They need, obviously, tons of exercise. Just looking at their physical type will tell you that. Lots of active games during learning will be the ticket to keeping your sight hound working happily and keeping his attention as well.

SCENT HOUNDS   Beagle, Basset Hound, Dachshund, Coonhound, Foxhound, Bloodhound, etc.

If the sight hounds are made of wind, the scent hounds are made of earth. They tend to be heavier and closer to the ground, more substantial of bone, immensely determined when on a scent.

Scent hounds tend to be slow to learn, easygoing, affable with other dogs, gentle and friendly with considerate children and very distracted by natural odors when out of doors. These dogs have unsuspicious natures and most are entirely unsuitable as watchdogs. Some tend to be noisy, even when not on the trail, and most scent hounds are difficult to housebreak.

Begin your training when your pup is still young to establish good habits early. Begin obedience work indoors to help you keep your hound's attention before trying to win it out of doors.

TOYS   Chihuahua, Toy Poodle, Yorkshire Terrier (a true terrier, but also a toy because of size), Papillon, Pug, Silky Terrier, Maltese, etc.

Toy dogs were bred not to work but to please. These charming little dogs are often spoiled rotten, carried around like toys and not educated at all. But inside each small package there is a real dog with a sharp and clever mind as capable of education—or troublemaking—as any other dog of any size. All toy dogs should be carefully housebroken *and* obedience trained. Untrained, toy dogs tend to be obnoxious. Untrained, toy dogs tend to be bored stiff. These dogs make great obedience competitors and trained, socialized and treated like dogs, they make easy, interesting pets.

HERDING BREEDS   Collie, German Shepherd Dog, Shetland Sheepdog, Old English Sheepdog, Australian Cattle Dog, Puli, Briard, Corgi, Border Collie, etc.

Among the herding breeds are the German Shepherd dog (*shep-herd*, from the Old English word for sheep herder) and the Collie, so you know that the dogs in this group are capable of higher education. These dogs bond well to families, are naturally protective and love to work. They need exercise and discipline, like any other dogs. Unless you have a flock, their herding instincts should be monitored and gently directed into active game playing. Do not put your herding dog into the yard with a bunch of little kids unless you want all the kids standing in a tight little circle in one corner of the yard. Herding dogs tend to nip at the ankles in order to direct traffic, so always remember your dog's hidden agenda, his work function. Work with it and around it, but don't forget about it, because your dog can't.

CANINE CHARACTER TYPES

Is your dog a character? Of course he is. But which one?

THE SMART DOG   She understands everything. Sometimes you think she understands English. If you close a door, she'll figure out how to open it. If you play a game, she's a step or a rule ahead of you. She's clever, too. She cracks jokes. And she can manipulate like nobody else.

She gets bored and when she's bored, she longs for fun. She might make fun by making trouble. She thinks, okay, let's see what this turkey will do if I *don't* sit. The smart dog finds it easy to get the best of you. The smart dog will keep you on your toe nails. Solution: Be smarter than your dog.

Teach the smart dog via interesting, complicated games. Change your pattern. Take her to different environments for training. Keep expecting more from her. Don't keep going over the same old stuff. Instead, add new twists and make the work interesting and challenging.

THE DUMB DOG   He's a challenge because he takes so long to learn anything new. Ten times you do a sit-stay. Ten times the dog follows you as you leave him. He's exasperating. Who can put up with all the boring repetition it requires to train a dumb dog? Instead of giving up, break everything up into little pieces for him. First do sit without stay. When you teach stay, stand right in front of him. Next, take one step backward. Work slowly toward standing a full leash length away from him when he does a stay. Make the distance shorter if you find he's breaking because you're going too fast for him.

Be patient. A slow-to-learn dog still needs to be trained and, smart or dumb, the more you teach him, the faster and better he'll learn. Keep in mind that the so-called dumb dog is probably a smart dog when he's doing what he was bred to do. Just because

you want him to do something else and he doesn't pick it up that quickly is no reason to deprive him of an education. Ninety percent of the time when an owner tells me his dog is dumb, the problem is not the dog's intelligence but the owner's failure to communicate with his dog. If this book can help change your mind about your dog's IQ and enable you to have fun and success teaching him, my effort will have been worthwhile. It bothers me to see someone give up on reaching his dog before he has barely given education a try. The thing that fascinates me most about dogs is their willingness to try to communicate with another species and the simply wonderful glimpses of canine intelligence and humor we humans can get when we make the effort to understand and communicate with them. So if you think your dog is dumb, please think again.

THE HIGH-ENERGY DOG He'd love to work, to obey, to sit still. But he can't. He's got ants in his pants. He can't concentrate. He can't stay. He can't take the time to look you in the eye. Above all, he can't hear you. He's Mr. Machine and he never stops.

The high-energy dog needs training more than any other type, or your sanity goes AWOL. Don't let him learn to use his high energy to get away with anything. Don't let him appear to "forget" he's working. Get eye contact. Get him to *stop, look* and *listen*. Be sure to exercise him before, after and during his training sessions.

THE STUBBORN DOG He was born to test your patience. He's not a dumb dog, though when he fails to obey you you may think he's doing it because he's dumb. Instead, something in him makes him want to do it his way. Wildly different types of dogs can be stubborn about getting educated. Some of the Spitz breeds, in their desire to function as they please, not as you please, will seem stubborn. But so are terriers. We know they have to be for the work they were originally bred to do. The average sporting dog may test you two or three times. The terrier will test you twenty times and have enough energy left for twenty more. The Boxer is a stubborn dog. He'll learn quickly and then, for fun and control, remove a skill or two. It's as if he's thinking, "Okay, you want the heel today. Fine. I'll give you the heel and take away the sit-stay."

Stubborn dogs need stubborn owners. Know you are smarter than your dog. (You're reading, aren't you?) And know you've got to win and you can. The stubborn dog, the dumb dog, the clever and smart dog, none of these animals can know that education is the key to their freedom and their happiness. But you know that, so no matter which work-stopping technique the stubborn dog tosses in your way, work around it and keep on going until your dog is safely and nicely trained.

THE INDEPENDENT DOG   She can be of any breed, as can the stubborn dog, and she's considerably more interested in pleasing herself than she is in pleasing you. Good news! You can *teach* a dog to focus on you more than she does naturally. By encouraging your dog to always come for praise after you release her from command, you will accustom her to expect and even enjoy getting your approval. If yours is an independent teenager and walks off when you tell her, "Okay," insist, with a leash if necessary, that she comes for praise before she leaves on her daily adventure.

Encourage the independent dog to look *to* you for affection and approval and to respect your disapproval as well. You won't be turning a Basenji into a Golden Retriever. You will be socializing your dog to make her a more interactive member of your family.

THE LETHARGIC DOG   This dog would love to cooperate with you but he's too pooped. He'll sit-stay for you, right after his nap. In fact, when you take this customer to obedience class or out to work, he's out to lunch. He yawns when you give him a command. He lies down and snores when you want him to get up and heel. He's a tired boy, a mess.

Some dogs, because of body weight and size, are difficult to get moving. So your job with the Bulldog or Newfoundland who doesn't want to move faster than a crawl is to motivate the dog to keep going. Do this with a cheerful, energetic voice, clapping, tapping your leg as you walk, baiting with a favorite ball or toy, running, even slowly if you must, to get your dog going. Do not slow down to match your slow-moving dog's pace, but work at getting him to move up to yours.

I once trained a Bulldog puppy who would not come out of his crate for lessons unless he was dragged out. It's not that he disliked training. He wouldn't even come out for a play session or his dinner. He was a tired dog. At least the down-stay was a snap!

Be careful with the dog who seems lethargic, especially if he's still a youngster. He may have a medical problem that, for example, makes him short of oxygen. If your dog *always* seems tired, have your veterinarian check him out. But lethargy can be a learned response. A coincidence (one day when you try to give him a training session he's really too tired), body type (low and weighty), or a character trait (slow moving, unexcitable) can also inspire a learned response, making a dog *act* lethargic to get his way. So if he's tough to get moving and the veterinarian says he's perfectly healthy, get him up and out and moving anyway.

THE HUGE DOG This animal may use a passive-aggressive mode to stop the work, the action or even your heart. At the drop of a command, he will turn himself into a bag of cement and sink to the ground. He may even give you that infuriating let's-see-you-get-me-back-up, turkey look! This is a tough problem for small or weak people with big dogs. But you *must* get your bag of cement on his feet and back to work. If you do not convince him that you can indeed haul his weight around, you'll never get him to obey you. You may even have trouble getting enough room to ever sleep in your own bed! So—wear old clothes, a look of determination and lots of deodorant. This is sweaty work, but once it's done, your adolescent giant will listen to you. Try to do this *before* he finishes "filling out," or, as a less-polite person might say, "porking up!"

The huge dog may have the following favorite way to stop a training lesson. You better know about this game I call sack-o'-potatoes because if he plays it, you'll have to win at it. You put your dog on a sit-stay. Instead of staying in the sitting position, the dog, often locking eyes with you first, slowly slides into the down. Now, almost every dog will lie down on the sit-stay when you first teach it. This is how you know he understands the *stay* part. He's merely trying to get comfortable. But since the basic commands are arbitrary and only as such can they potentially save your dog's life in case of danger, your response should be, "No, sit." Then tug upward on the leash and remind the dog what *sit* means. With the dog who is playing sack-o'-potatoes, he has not just learned to lie down on a sit-stay, he has also figured out that he can use his weight as a weapon. In doing so, he is challenging you to do something about it. I am sorry to report that you must. I have used everything short of a derrick to reposition larger-than-life dogs into the sit, knowing all along that they would slide back down the minute I stepped away. The good news is that you can accomplish what you must by winning this battle several times during a single training session. This will convince the big brute that you can physically handle him despite his size. If you call in the marines—bigger, stronger family members to help you—the dog will listen to them but never to you.

I once had a smallish ten-year-old boy come to one of my group classes with an Irish Wolfhound. They were a ridiculous combination and I told his mother the dog would never get well trained. "No problem," she said. "This is for *him*, not her." So I accepted the small boy and huge dog team—knowing full well that first day that he would have to play and win some version of sack with his dog in order to convince her that he was boss. As it turned out, she played a reverse version of the game. She refused to lie down on command. I stood by, along with the rest of the class, as this gutsy kid struggled to get his big girl to lie down. I could have easily stepped in. But she was smart enough to know exactly what that action would signify.

The young man was very determined and very courageous. He was the only child in an adult class and he had the biggest dog. At the end of the ten-week course, my young friend had the best-trained dog. Winning at sack, as he had done, offers a stunning reward, no matter which version of the game your dog plays.

THE FAST DOG   This animal works so quickly that when you give a command, you may actually miss the dog's execution of it. Slow the dog down by demanding precise work at your pace. But even though you will teach him to *sometimes* walk slowly with you, fast is better than slow and far better than not at all. So do an occasional long down and get eye contact from him, but don't bore him to death by asking him to be somebody he isn't.

THE SLOW DOG   If you are unhappy with a fast dog, read about the slow dog. You won't want to trade.

The slow dog, like the lethargic dog, may hope *you'll* nod off or give up while you're waiting. You can speed these dogs up. Trust me. Teach some fun doggy games and keep the play very lively. Even a slow-moving dog will *play* with some amount of zest and speed, sometimes a downright surprising amount. Once you've seen a faster version of your slow teen through play, begin to shuffle work and play as you would a deck of cards. Mixing the work into the play and vice versa will confuse the dog in the loveliest way. If it was his (or your) bad attitude about work which slowed him down, his (and your) good attitude about play will now speed him up.

I once had a darling Sussex Spaniel puppy in an outdoor group training class. Because the class was held in a park and all the dogs played there anyway, we knew they'd come back when called from their play breaks. So we'd work for twenty or thirty minutes and then stand around and watch our dogs go wild and play for the next twenty or thirty minutes. Then we'd call them back and finish the class.

The little Sussex boy ran around and had a terrific time during the play period, but during class time, he literally schlepped. His head hung low, his big feet dragged. I kept trying to get his owner to put a little oomph in his voice, but I couldn't seem to get this dog *up*. Then one day I noticed that the Sussex Spaniel's owner had the same hangdog look and foot-dragging walk as his puppy. Yet he brightened up at playtime, just like his pup.

We began to teach more and more through play and soon enough both owner and dog were working in a happier fashion and at a quicker pace. So when you are trying to excite your slow-moving dog, take a moment to examine your own feelings about obedience training. If you think it's mean to train your dog, even a speedy dog will schlep and look miserable. Sometimes the answer is not in the dog but in the master!

THE TINY DOG   Could isms cowwect a cute wittle dawg wike me? You bet your little coat and booties I could and have and do! The temptation to let a teeny, tiny, small dog bamboozle you is almost irresistible. But I have seen too many teeny, tiny, small Napoleons to find this syndrome cute.

If you have a little dog and you ask him to do something, make him do it. Even though *he* may think he's a Mastiff, you won't need a whip and a chair. But do use a buckle collar, not a slip collar, and a leash. You won't break him. You'll merely educate him. And little dogs love to work and show off, sometimes even more than big ones.

THE SICK OR INJURED DOG   Such a dog will learn quickly how to feign illness or injury when he's perfectly well. It's a foolproof method for getting out of work. Drop a command and your dog will fall into bed and run a fever. She'll vomit, limp, and appear to slip into a coma. So you must know your dog. If she has ever been sick or injured and during that time *of course* you let her sleep on the couch and you never made her do anything, watch and see if she's added the sickness game to her repertoire of ways to stop you from training her. This kind of behavior usually occurs during adolescence when dogs so much want to get their own way. I have seen *everything* tried in obedience class, including a dog who never limped all week but who limped every Thursday night from eight to nine! The owner, by the way, refused to believe the limp was fake until on the third lesson the dog forgot an important detail of her own routine and switched legs.

THE AGGRESSIVE DOG   The truly aggressive dog is a tough customer and if you have one and he's already an adolescent, you'd do best to hire a professional trainer, preferably one who has been highly recommended to you. However, not all dogs who act grouchy and growly when you try to train them are *truly* aggressive. Some are dogs who have learned that growls, stares and fierce behavior scare off their owners and stop the training. This allows them to do just as they please. And that's a result they like.

How will you know if your dog is seriously aggressive or if he's using an aggressive mode to get his way? You already know, don't you? Most owners know if their dog is a rotten apple or merely a rotten brat. If you don't, hire a trainer. You don't want to take a chance with a bite.

But if you are pretty sure that your dog is just acting the bully to prevent you from being in charge, then ignore his nonsense and train away. Hint: Does he avoid eye contact or stare? If he stares, hire a trainer. If he avoids eye contact, he's probably just not willing to let you be his leader. If the latter, a good obedience course should do the trick. Train matter of factly, planning each lesson beforehand and following your plan each time you train. Do not back down when the dog rumbles and grumbles. Use a leash and get your way. If the dog stops heeling, digs in and looks mean, shrug your shoulders, give him a quick pop on the leash and keep on going. If you refuse to take a bully seriously, it takes the wind out of his sails pronto. In any case, never let your dog scare you off or make you back down. If you need the help of a professional, get help, otherwise your dog will become more and more aggressive. In other words, he'll make use of whatever succeeds for him.

THE WIMP   The wimp has a great routine. You correct her and she falls apart. She cowers, cringes, falls over, urinates, paws in your direction from the ground. How pitiful-looking can you get! The wimp has it all down pat.

Does your dog make you feel like a beast every time she's naughty and you try to make a correction? After all, how can you correct a dog who's trembling and begging for mercy. And, oh, how the wimp can dramatize! If a mild, justified correction makes your dog suicidal, you may be spending your hard-earned bucks supporting a manipulative creature. Ignore the display and continue to go about the business of training your dog in a cheerful, brisk manner. Whatever doesn't work, a dog will drop.

THE RING-WISE DOG   If you compete in the sport of obedience and your dog is perfect when you practice and highly imperfect in the ring where rules say you cannot make a correction, you probably have a ring-wise dog. You take your dog to class where practice makes perfect and where you can correct him if he goofs and you get good attention and instant obedience. You sign up for an obedience trial and your dog turns into a comedian in the ring, stopping in the middle of heeling, standing up on the long down, leaving the ring. Now why would a nice dog do something like that? Is your adolescent dog just too immature for the pressure you and he feel when competing? Is your relationship all about getting a qualifying ribbon or a high score and not enough about mutual respect, admiration and affection? Is your dog simply not trained or socialized enough to work well in a strange area? Nice dogs don't mess you up for no reason. Take a month off from training and make friends with your dog on long hikes, picnics and through game playing. Then begin again, but less obsessively, more slowly and with lots of fun games added. The ring-wise dog is usually a relationship problem and the time off and new attitude should solve the problem nicely.

Figuring out your dog's method for gaining the upper hand does not mean you're winning against an enemy. Your dog is your friend. But he is a dog. And so it's natural for him to try to get his way and take his time. Understanding how he goes about this and having the satisfaction of getting things done your way can only make for a better, richer relationship with the dog you love.

6

TRADE SECRETS

Now that we have examined many ways your dog might behave because of his instincts, breed type or particular set of character traits, we need to discuss *your* behavior when you are working and playing with your dog. Don't run away. This is not going to be a lecture from your mother. Quite the contrary. Here now are the trade secrets of professional trainers—ways to have more fun and more success as you teach. Here now are twenty-plus years' worth of big and little secrets to speed the work, make it more efficient, make your relationship with your wonderful, energetic, bratty dog more pleasurable for both of you.

TRICKS OF
THE TRADE

Plan for today *and* for the future

Having realistic goals will help you train patiently and intelligently. Thinking ahead to the way you'd like your dog to be as an adult will help you plan the small steps you will have to take over the next several months to lead him in the right direction. When he's *finally* grown up, shall he be obedient off-leash on voice and/or hand signals, calm when company comes, a safe, fun companion for children, the affable performer of a few dazzling but dignified tricks, a peach around other dogs? Fine. Plan how you're going to get there. Plot out each step that will help you have the dog you want. Don't do anything in early training that will spoil it for your larger goal.

You'll want a goal for each lesson. This is particularly important with an adolescent dog whose personality may seem to change from one day to the next. On a good day, you may try a new command or you may want to string two commands together so that your dog starts to work more smoothly. On a bad day, it may take you the whole lesson to get your dog's attention for a mere moment. That can be a good day's work with an adolescent dog. Use that precious moment by doing a sit-stay or a little heeling, then head for the park and pray for other friendly dogs.

A daily plan gives your lesson a central focus. Of course, you'll do other work with your dog, too. But once you get *one* good response to your main goal, a terrific automatic sit or an ungrouchy down in a store, praise the dog to the sky and end the session with a game. You probably should plan a learning game (even during playtime, a dog is learning) as part of each daily lesson, to keep motivation high for both of you and to end each lesson having fun.

No matter what your daily goal is, always communicate to your dog when work is to begin. Do this with a simple sit-stay. Then "warm him up" with some fast heeling, some turns to keep his attention, a few stops and one or two down-stays. Next begin to work on your project for the day, using every trick in the book to get good results. If you wish to speed up his recall, call him and run backwards. Make him work to get to you. Play some recall games, too, calling him back and forth between two of his favorite people. Praise a lot. Praise warmly. And forgo the automatic sit in favor of speed for a while. Instead, try a surprising breakaway from him, calling, "Come, come, come," as you run away, holding the leash, of course. When he runs straight to you, praise and don't push on to see if he'll do it again. His reward for work well done is an end to that work for that day.

Make notes

After each lesson, make notes about what your dog does well, badly, not at all. Write down what you did to reach your goal and how close you came. Immediately plan tomorrow's lesson—what you plan to work on, where you plan to go for the practice session, what games and exercises you think would help. You'll be thrilled when you can easily remind yourself what you achieved the lesson before and then continue along with what you planned to teach next at a time when the previous lesson is still fresh in your mind.

Always take the time to reestablish yourself as alpha

No professional trainer worth her salt would begin a training session without first establishing that she was in charge. If you are working indoors, a long down will get your point across nicely. It calms a dog, too, so his mind is clearer and he's easier to reach. If you're out of doors, try a sit-stay in the face of distractions. Once your dog will hold this command where there's some action— kids on bikes, other dogs passing, lots of people—you'll have his respect and will be able to work properly. Take a moment, while your dog is on his down or sit-stay to make friendly eye contact with him. Without his attention, how can you begin a training session?

Often people will come to me with a dog who looks frantically from side to side. Everything but the owner grabs this dog's attention. As a result, the dog appears to be a nervous wreck. By learning to focus on his owner, a dog calms down and is in a frame of mind for work. He no longer has to check out everything in the world that moves. He understands that his owner is in charge and that his owner will make sure that everything is okay. This frees the dog to concentrate on you and to relax. The only way to begin a lesson is to check to see that the relationship is in good shape by seeing if the dog will stop, look and listen before you proceed with your plan for the day.

Concentrate on one problem at a time

You can review old work, but, basically, deal with one problem at a time: a crooked sit, naughty jumping up, forging ahead. In this way, your focus is clearer and you are less likely to quit prematurely or confuse your dog. Also, if the problem you are dealing with requires some firm leash corrections, you should keep the rest of the lesson lighter and brighter. It's important for both you and the dog that most of the lesson is comprised of positive achievements, things done well and appreciated. No dog can get too much praise for doing his work well.

Make believe the dog isn't yours

When I can't solve a problem with one of my dogs, I pretend a potential client has called and described this very behavior. Then I can quickly figure out exactly what to do and, just as important, what to stop doing. If you can't get your dog trained because you're much too attached—and who isn't!—forget that he's yours, at least for the moment. It really can be difficult to view your own dog dispassionately, but sometimes the need to educate him or solve a behavior problem requires you to do just that. Pretend you're a professional trainer, working for a living and that this is a client's dog. It can give you instant twenty-twenty vision. We're all shortsighted with our own pets, yet we can see clearly what's wrong with other people's dogs.

Train a tired dog

If you sometimes think you need a forklift truck or a bulldozer instead of a leash, you are probably working your exuberant, energetic adolescent without exercising him. Mistake! Eventually, when he's grown up and mature (long-term goal), he should work well no matter what. But for now (short-term goal), be realistic. Give your dog a run for his money, *then* ask him to heel. If you

Train a tired dog.

try to work him when he's all pent up, you'll both get frustrated. Asking a dog to work after he's had some exercise makes more sense. It makes the job of training much easier and doing things the easy way can be great dog training. Eventually, when he's no longer an adolescent and you've gotten him pretty well trained, you can ask him to work even when he's not all in.

Teach and reward with play

One of the best ways to make sure a human student remembers a lesson is by using humor. The best way to make sure a dog is motivated to turn on his brain—particularly the adolescent dog who often seems to misplace that vital organ—is to teach via games and to reward good responses with play. Much of the teaching you will do following this guide will be couched in a game format. In addition, when you practice, save the last few minutes for a goofy game.

Let your dog teach you a few tricks

The observant dog owner will constantly be learning. If you are open, you can learn something new and fascinating each time you observe your dog playing with other dogs, each time you observe your dog's response to your teaching, each time you play a game with your dog. Keep your eye out for interesting reactions. Find out, by looking, what your dog is thinking, how he learns, how he tries to get away with things. Learning is a lifelong pleasure. Delight in what you can learn during time spent with your pet.

Keep your dog busy

One of my favorite editors once told me that he's sure he would have become a juvenile delinquent if his parents hadn't made him work after school. When his high school classes let out, he went straight to the supermarket and worked there until suppertime. After supper, he had to stay home and do his homework. He probably grumbled back then, but he's grateful now.

Your adolescent dog's energies should likewise be put to constructive use. Unfortunately, you will not be able to get him a job at Waldbaum's bagging groceries. But you can give him enough to do so that his mind and body will be tired at the end of each day. An adolescent dog—like an adolescent human—with too much spare time and not enough to do can be a disaster waiting to happen.

I take my dogs on long walks, take them to the park to play with other dogs, play interesting, active games, arrange play dates

Keep your dog busy.

with dog friends, give surprise training tune-ups, hide things for them to find, call them to follow me when I go for the mail or to the laundry room and, in general, try to keep them happily busy whenever I can. A dog, with the kind of bursts of energy adolescents have, left with not much to do, may make his own fun. While he probably won't hang around street corners smoking with his bad-influence friends, you probably will not like what he will do. A busy dog becomes a tired dog and a tired dog becomes a sleeping dog and there's nothing more pleasing to the owner of an adolescent dog than to see him asleep. In that way, you're more apt to say, "Doesn't he look like an angel when he sleeps!" than, "Oh, my God, what did he do now?"

Read your dog's standard, again

There's always something you've missed that will explain your dog to you in a way you didn't see before. Check and recheck to make sure you understand his breed function, that which determines his shape, his speed, his mind-set. Remember, with dogs, what you see is not what you get. You get more than meets the eye and one of the places to discover what that more is would be the standard. If you have a mixed-breed dog, you can still read. Is he a terrier type, a double coated Spitz, a heavy boned mastiff type, a Chihuahua crossed with a sesame seed? Read about his probable family. Read about breeds close to what he might be. Work backward, too. Observe the behavior and find the breeds that match it.

Warm hands, warm heart

Some people, when training their dogs, particularly when the dogs are in the throes of adolescence, end up in an adversarial relationship with their pets. This is the first thing I try to "fix" when I go out on a consultation. After all, most people obtain a pet dog thinking he will be a true companion, a buddy and, as the saying promises, your best friend. But your dog's behavior problems may inspire you to look at him as anything but a best friend. After all, best friends don't chew up your furniture, run away when you call them or growl at you when they are eating.

When you're feeling frustrated over your dog's behavior, take a moment to remember why you got him in the first place. When you do, you'll find it easier to train him and easier, too, to have the patience you need to work with an adolescent *anything*.

Now try this little trick that will make you and your dog feel good about each other again. Rub your hands together until they get very warm. Now ask your dog to sit. As soon as he obeys you by sitting, pet and praise him with both warm hands. Your dog will feel the warmth and energy in your hands as pure pleasure. It is almost as if the love you feel for him, that which you just reminded yourself of, is flowing to your dog right through your hands. You'll probably feel his love and gratitude right back. He may gaze into your eyes, or he may simply sigh and relax as you stroke his fur.

When you are working with your dog or playing with him, don't pet him timidly or tentatively. Give the dog a hug and stroke his fur firmly enough so that your hand gets warm *from* the petting. This better way to pet your dog will make him want to please you all the more.

Warm hands are good for puppies, too, to make them feel secure, and they're good for old dogs who need your loving touch more than ever. They're even good for the people you love. A pat on the back, to a dog or a person, always feels more loving when it is delivered by a warm hand.

Warm hands, warm heart.

Be creative

If your dog won't pay attention to you out of doors, even after sufficient exercise, hide a squeak toy in your pocket and tap your pocket every once in a while. Will he look to see where the high-pitched sound came from? Good. Praise him for looking. It's his attention you want, even if you have to be sneaky to get it.

Suppose you want to circle around behind your dog when he's on a sit-stay, just to make sure you can. The average teen will follow you with his head and soon enough, his whole body will follow. There you'll be, walking in a little circle with your dog walking behind you. Is he a dumb dog? No. He's a curious dog and furthermore, he truly doesn't understand what you want. As you approach his side, do what my friend the terrific dog trainer Captain Arthur Haggerty does. Gently lay one finger on the side of the dog's nose and keep it there as you circle him. The finger prevents his head from turning. Without turning his head, he'll stay put. This gentle, effective trick communicates in no time to the dog that when you circle behind him, he should hold his sit-stay. Beyond that, there's a larger message, as there almost always

Keep education interesting. Try working your teen with a favorite pal.

is in dog training. The real message is that when alpha gives a command and it is followed, no harm will come to the dog. He need not turn his head and follow you. He is safe and, like magic, you will show up promptly at his other side. From obedience comes trust, hence the bond between dog and master grows stronger.

Even if your adolescent dog doesn't seem to get it sometimes, keep working. By concentrating on him and inventing new ways to reach and teach him, eventually the job will get done. Don't be afraid to try new things. As long as they relate to the way his mother taught him, you will know that they will be both effective and humane.

Gentle is as gentle does

Here's a secret every dog owner should know. If you want to raise a nonaggressive dog, don't roughhouse or play tug-of-war. These games teach your dog to play too hard, to grab at things, to grasp firmly, to bite down hard. None of these traits bode well for pet dogs. For safety's sake, play active, but not rough.

Professional trainers know there's always something more to learn about dogs. If you work like a professional, using the secrets professional trainers use, you will not only be quicker and better at your task, you will be more receptive to learning, more content in the work, more appreciative of the learner—all worthy goals.

7

THE WAY
TO TRAIN

An important difference between a successful dog trainer, amateur or professional, and a less than successful one is the ability to pay attention. If you come to your dog full of anger because of his less than perfect behavior or full of ideas about control, about your mental and physical superiority, you are apt to miss the best part of having a dog in your care. Instead, if you approach your dog with an open mind and heart, you have the chance not only to do some beautiful, graceful teaching, you have the more valuable opportunity to be educated yourself.

There is much that we as a species have lost that dogs have retained. They do not have to go to shrinks to find out what they feel. They do not have to search long and hard for the child within. They do not waste precious, limited time longing for what they do not have or bemoaning the past. Your dog, as all dogs, lives fully in the present. He exhibits clearly, for any being receptive enough to look, all his emotions, emotions very similar to yours and mine. He has no puppy within. His puppy is right there. He can call upon it at any moment. He can be silly, playful, affectionate, full of wonder and humorous, all at the drop of a hat. Your dog can teach you to be more like him. He can help you to be a more content human being.

If you come empty rather than full to a training session, leaving some room within in which to learn as well as teach, your dog will teach you how to educate him. You need not rush to train, even if you are a trainer by profession. Take the time to observe each dog and from your observation and your hesitation to form opinions, see what he is telling you about himself and about the world. If you learn to do this, you will not only succeed at training dogs, you will be rich indeed.

In order to understand the information available every time you look at your dog or any other dog, first make yourself still and quiet. When I go to someone's home to train his dog, I usually greet the dog warmly and briefly and then sit down quietly in a chair and observe what he does. As I listen to his owners describe his behavior problems as they perceive them, I watch the way the dog reacts to a stranger, me, and the way he "works" his owners, asking for reassurance or a game, retreating to sleep so that he does not have to deal with me, acting aggressive to chase me away, or trying to charm the whole household in order to maintain control. Before I touch the leash, I have learned a lot about how to teach from my student.

If, on the other hand, you are *sure* that your dog's annoying adolescent behavior is spiteful, or that he hasn't learned because he is dumb, not because you haven't communicated clearly and appropriately to him, you probably won't be a terribly successful teacher this time around either.

Education is available each time you see your dog react to anything, to you, to another dog, to the great outdoors or a new toy, to what's on TV, to rain or snow. When you begin to train, note each tiny detail of what your dog does in response to you. Quietly ask yourself what each thing means. There'll be some practice doing this when we get to the training pictures in this chapter, because each dog photographed will not only obey or disobey, he

Sit and down are two separate commands.

will also display his character in the way he reacts to the training and the trainer.

An important difference between a trained dog and an untrained dog, besides the willingness or lack of same to obey commands, is his ability to pay attention. Your dog must stop, look and listen in order to find out what it is you are asking him to do. The sit-stay is one way to teach him how to do this. In addition, you can help him learn quickly by speaking to him in a clear, simple way. The more consistent and terse you are when you are in the process of training your dog, the better. Long sentences, even paragraphs, said or sung, are fine when what you want to do is express feeling to your dog. But for training, one or two words at a time work best.

Be precise and use the same word for the same action every time. Never use a double command such as sit down. *Sit* and *down* are two separate commands. No wonder the dog is confused and the owner needs to hire a dog trainer! You can save yourself a lot of money by using the same word, *sit* or *down* or *come*, each time you want your dog to perform that task.

It is also important to be perfectly clear about your likes and dislikes. You must monitor the dog's behavior and let him know which activities garner your approval and which are no-no's. The way to do this is with the two most important words in any dog's vocabulary, *okay* and *no*.

The two most important words in any dog's vocabulary are no . . .

and okay.

OKAY GIVES PERMISSION

Okay is a release word. It means your dog can do whatever he wants to: Get up from his sit-stay, stop heeling and start sniffing, eat from the pan you just placed on the floor, get up from his down-stay, get in or out of the car.

Some of my clients complicate the job of educating their dogs by using the word *okay* before every command. They say, "Okay, heel," or "Okay, sit." If you have this habit, try to break it. It is terribly confusing to the dog and hell on his training. Instead, use okay as consistently and precisely as if it were a command.

Teaching okay couldn't be easier. Dogs learn the meaning instantly because the reward is built right in—do as you please. Here's the easiest way to teach it. Fill your dog's dinner bowl. Ask him to sit. (Even if he doesn't know the sit, he'll figure it out if you are holding his dinner.) After he sits, tell him okay as you place the bowl down in front of him. As he begins to eat, let him know he is both correct and brilliant by saying, "Good boy." He now knows the command okay and you can use it as one of the ways you release him from another command or give him permission to do something.

JUST SAY NO

Many of the problems I hear about from friends and clients with adolescent dogs have to do with ever more creative naughty behavior, things that crop up as the dog tests and tests in order to understand where his boundaries are. The complaint is voiced and I always counter with, "What did you do?" Almost always, the answer is, "Nothing."

When your adolescent dog jumps on the bed at six in the morning, puts his paws on the table and begins to eat out of your plate, begins to chew on the shoe you just slipped off, barks and barks for attention, keeps tossing toys on your lap when you don't want to play, acts aggressive toward someone at your door, steals your underwear, tugs at your bathrobe, just say no. *No* might not be enough in some cases, though in a surprising number of them it is. But it is always the way to begin a dialogue with your dog when he is doing something you do not want him to do. After all, if you do not teach him your likes and dislikes, how is he to know what he can and can't do? Properly voiced, said seriously, said in a deep rather than a high voice and said once, no is a powerful correction, resonating naturally with the *grrrr* his mother used when he was a cheeky little puppy and pulled too hard on her ears or tail.

LET'S GO TO THE MOVIES

Since a picture is worth more than ten thousand words, particularly when the picture demonstrates the training of a naughty, inattentive adolescent dog, the way to train will be demonstrated visually. In this way, I hope you will be able to *see* the force or gentleness of a correction, the intensity of praise, the correct position for dog and master, the attentiveness we are after, and some illuminating examples of a range of intermediary reactions to training, many of which you may find amusing simply because they are being demonstrated by someone else's dog.

First, let's see how to "dress" the dog for training and how to praise and correct him.

How to Praise

A hug is a terrific way to praise your good dog.

*How to Put on a
Training Collar*

*Slip the collar through one of the
loops, forming a "P," then simply
slip the "P" over the dog's head.
(Note that trainer is standing on
Lucy's leash to insure 100 percent
safety. No adolescent dog is 100
percent reliable when off-leash out of
doors. Don't take chances
with your baby.)*

*The collar comes
over Lucy's neck,
ready to be attach-
ed to her leash.*

How to Hold the Leash

Fold the excess leash neatly and hold your arms in a relaxed, comfortable way.

How to Correct

When necessary, correct with a small, quick tug followed by an immediate release.

Now let's get down to basics, basic commands, that is. Here is the vocabulary you need to live safely and sanely with any dog. Commands should be said once in a normal voice, not shouted, not said as if there were a question mark after each. When the dog obeys, he should be praised warmly. At first, praise should be immediate. In this way, the dog understands what he did that was so terrific. As you work, praise may be delayed until after an exercise is completed. In other words, if you place your dog on a sit-stay, do not praise him until after you break the stay. If you praise him in the middle, for staying so well, he will probably think he is finished working and break.

You are the only one who should break a command. If your dog can break the sit-stay, why can't he disobey when you call come? For your dog's safety, these few commands are arbitrary in nature and must be obeyed. That is, you get to choose which thing the dog should do and he must sit or come or lie down, just as you say. Even lying down on a sit-stay is breaking. If he can do that, to repeat an important question, why can't he disobey when you call come? Get it?

So what should you do when your dog breaks a command, the adolescent specialty? Simply correct him. Do not get angry. Do not decide he's dumb. In fact, breaking and getting corrected is how he actually learns what it is he should be doing.

Exactly what is a correction? It could be a warning no. It could be a pop and release with the leash. It could mean marching a dog back to where he was and repeating a command. It could mean using the leash to replace a dog in a sit or a down and *not* repeating

Breaking and getting corrected is how your dog learns.

the command, because after a couple of corrections, you can assume the dog remembers which command he keeps on breaking.

Always try the mildest correct first—no. It often works. If your
dog begins to lie down on a sit-stay exercise, you may want
your mild correction to be more specific—no, sit! The no means
your dog did something he shouldn't have. He broke the sit to lie
down. The sit reminds him once more what he should be doing.
He may correct himself. If not, pull up on the leash, repeating sit.
Or, if the dog weighs a ton, get him up by walking and then take
him back to the same spot and put him back in a sit.

If you want your dog to learn to listen and obey a few basic
commands, correct him whenever he breaks with the mildest correction that is effective. Do not keep using a correction that fails
to work. If no doesn't get your dog to obey, you must use a leash
correction, usually a quick tug and release. Also, do not break the
dog because you see he is about to break or actually starting to
break. No dog is so dumb he won't see through that little trick.
Even if you were just about to say okay, if the dog breaks, say
no, and wait another ten seconds before offering him a cheerful,
enthusiastic okay. Make sure your okay is always audible and full
of energy. Make sure your praise is sufficient to motivate your
dog to please you again. Always, always be sure the dog comes
for and receives warm praise after you break him. Do not let him
walk off in a huff after he hears okay. The more he learns to come
to you for praise after working, the more his positive focus will
be on you as leader and as friend. Now we're ready to roll.

Do not keep using a correction that fails to work.

Sit

In order to teach your dog to sit on command, you can attract him to look up by holding his favorite toy over his head.

Angus sits in order to look up more easily. Try to use the command sit *just as he starts to sit. Praise immediately.*

Or, you can say sit as you pull up on the leash and push down on the rump. Don't forget to praise.

Stay

Swing your hand toward your dog's face, saying "Stay." Once he's steady, go back a step or two.

Keep your hand under the leash so that if your dog should start to break, you can lift the leash for a small, swift, effective correction as you say "No, stay."

And he will, as Angus does.

With practice,
he'll stay and
watch you calmly.

An underconfident dog may appear frightened the first time she's asked to work out of doors.

A cockier dog might try to stop a training lesson with the message that training is duller than dishwater. We are not deterred.

But if, despite her fears, she's told to stay, her comfort and confidence will increase in time. Good girl, Blue!

Even when something more interesting captures Dexter's attention, when asked to stay, stay he must.

Release your dog from his sit-stay with a cheerful okay.

And don't forget to praise.

Come

Begin teaching the recall from the sit-stay. Swing your arm out to the side and then back in toward your chest as you call out cheerfully, "Holden, come."

Gather up the leash as he comes in.

Good boy, come! (If you want to speed the recall, you can run backward as you playfully call your dog to come. Every dog wants what it seems he cannot have!)

After he arrives and sits, tell him he's the best dog that was ever born. And mean it!

Heel

Begin teaching the heel with your dog sitting at your left side.

Telling him "Jake, heel," begin to walk, left leg (the one he's near) moving out first.

Hold his attention by making turns, tapping your leg to remind him where he should be.

If he pulls ahead, lags behind, strays out to the side or if his attention flags (It will. He's a teen!), add a quick tug . . .

followed by an immediate release. Continue on, praising as you go. With daily practice, five or ten minutes at a time, you'll teach your dog how to heel. Truly!

Always get a sit when you stop and always praise warmly after he sits.

End as you began—in the heel position. Then praise again, "Good boy, Jake!" and give him his release word, "Okay." Never let your dog simply stop working on his own without a release from you.

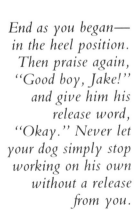

Down

Many dogs, even during the terrible teens, will lie down for a favorite toy. Start with the sit-stay and draw the toy down and forward, saying "Down" as you do.

Good boy, Dexter!

Others will need assistance to go into the down position. Gently lift his legs.

Gently place them down. Good boy!

Pat the floor when you give the command down.

Tell him "Stay," just as you did on the sit-stay. As you practice, increase the time you require your dog to stay down.

Release him with okay and let him come to you for his hug.

As he catches on to the basic commands, have him work with his playmates. Sit, fellows. Stay. Good puppies!

Down, Stay! Practice makes perfect.

Oops. Eventually . . .

DEALING WITH EMERGENCIES

Unlike a computer, which does precisely what it has been programmed and instructed to do, a dog can and may use his fiercely
interesting little mind or, in the case of an adolescent dog, his
mercurial emotions, to come up with a solution or result other
than the one you think you programmed in and instructed him to
perform. Because of this, and because I am a responsible human
being who truly loves dogs, this chapter on how to train cannot
be considered complete without a sort of accident insurance policy
to cover your dog's safety. A dog's world is full of tempting booby
traps: Rabbits to chase, playmates across the street, trails to follow,
scents to explore, swimming holes to find or, Heaven help you, a
female in heat. An open door, a dropped or broken leash, a collar
that suddenly slips off, a dog who's fast enough to slip out of the
car before you get a chance to say stay—an accidentally loose dog
can become a lost dog, an injured dog or, too sad for words, a
dead dog.

Not all potential dangers can be safely guarded against. Some
day someone is bound to forget to shut the door properly and a
leash can slip out of a gloved hand without your knowing it right
away. Even the dog who lives in a wonderfully safe kennel and
rides to dog shows in his crate might one day take off when his
show lead snaps or when he sees, for the first time in his life, a
truly irresistible temptation, backs out of his collar and disappears.
What's a concerned owner to do?

Preparing for the emergency you hope will never happen is the
best way to protect your dog from loss or injury. In this way,
even if the slip collar slips off, the leash gets dropped, someone
leaves a door or gate unlatched, you will have a set of commands
as well as other tricks up your sleeve that will help you get your
dog to turn around and return safely to your arms. Take the time,
after you have taught the basic commands, to prepare yourself and
your precious dog for the just-in-case you hope will never occur.

DRAG IT If you are walking your dog and you drop the leash,
he might take off. (Attention owners of Nordic breeds: Your dog
will take off.) How about if he doesn't know right away that you
dropped the leash? After all, there's no law that says you can't be

just as sneaky as your dog. Next time you take your dog out, let go of everything except the handle of the leash, allowing the rest of the leash to go slack, touch the ground and drag for a moment. Say nothing and resume your normal hold on the leash. Your dog, depending on how bad a runner he is, may try to take off the very first time you try this. Surprise! He will be caught short with a self-given correction. After a time, he will pay no attention at all to the feel of the leash on the ground. This important safety trick gives you the several seconds you'd need to pick up or step on a dropped leash.

WAIT! I can let little kids walk my sweet Shepherd, Scarlet, because if the leash is dropped, she stops. "Wait" is a great safety command.

I always teach my dogs to wait before crossing the street, to stop them from charging forward into traffic. Of course, they are on-leash anyway. But stopping at the curb becomes a habit, too. Wait can also give you your dog's attention when he is about to do a disappearing act. The dog who fully understands that come means he's going back on-leash, into the car or into the crate or kennel may be reluctant to do so. But calling out "Wait" may give him pause. An assertive "Down" would be an excellent follow up—and would give you a much better chance to recover a runaway than would a straight recall.

If you want your dog to stop should the leash accidentally drop, practice in a safe area—indoors at first or in a fenced-in area. Walk the dog around on a leash. Let go of the leash and say "Wait." If the dog ignores you and continues to move around, grasp the collar, or step on the leash and repeat the command *wait* as you make the correction. Practicing this will accustom the dog to stopping when the leash drops, a safety feature nearly as good as a car's airbag.

THE EMERGENCY DOWN   Every dog should know the emergency down. Instructions for teaching it are in Chapter Three. If you have not taught it because your dog did not respond to the down-stay command, you can teach it now. Since you cannot teach your dog everything at once, the way you can install a complete program into a computer, be especially cautious about his safety until he responds immediately to this command. The emergency down, which requires an immediate response and thus can save your dog's life when he's headed for danger or even just away, teaches your dog to obey instantly without thinking. After all, while a dog is thinking over whether or not to obey, he could get killed. The next exercise teaches him to obey you *after* thinking. In other words, it teaches him to use his head.

HEEL FROM A DISTANCE After your dog has learned to heel, begin to stop, signal him to stay, proceed (right leg moving first) to the end of his leash and then, saying his name and "Heel," tap your left leg to attract him to his place and continue walking as he catches up. After practicing this for several weeks, try getting him to come to heel from various angles and from a greater distance, and eventually, if he is trustworthy, off-leash. The dog that has it in his head that come means the fun is over often will "come" to heel from a distance.

YOU CAN'T FIRE ME, I QUIT Let us be brave and deal with the loose dog who just will not come. You've tried wait, down, heel, come, stay and every curse word you know. Nothing. You can see your dog. But he won't approach you and if you try to approach him, he takes off. Give the recall one more try. Bend, hold your arms way out to the side, lovingly and cheerfully (yes, you can!), call his name and sing, "Come." If this fails (it often works), sit on the ground—or just crouch if it's wet out—hide your face in your hands and pretend to cry, loudly. By now you probably want to anyway. If a minute of boo-hooing doesn't get a cold wet nose poking under your hands, try whining and whimpering like a puppy. This almost always gets them!

Okay, here's the you-can't-fire-me-I-quit part. You've tried everything. You're fed up. You're scared. You're late for work. Get up, dust yourself off, and hooting to get your dog's attention, run in the opposite direction from where he is. If *this* doesn't bring your dog running, consider saving up for a more obedient breed!

LEAVE IT! There's one more emergency command that could save your dog's life, yet it has nothing to do with running away. A reliable response to the command *leave it* could mean your dog would drop something dangerous from his mouth or even ignore an aggressive dog he was approaching. I am amazed to see how wonderfully well this works when I take my puppy to the dog run and use it to warn him off another male who might find his friendly advances annoying.

Even if you chose your breed for its ability to protect you, there are circumstances where you need to be the protector. Preparing for emergencies and teaching safety commands may be among the most important things you do for your dog.

Part
Three

"Man plans, God laughs."

YIDDISH PROVERB

8

GUERRILLA
WARFARE

Keeping your dog problem-free or figuring out and correcting the problems he may already have is more a matter of what you *are* than of what you *do*. Once you have garnered your dog's true respect, many of the problems you previously fretted over will begin to abate and his behavior will fall into line. There will be times, however, when you will need to practice swift, stunning intervention, to monitor, to correct, to train and retrain. This part of the book will help you to know what to do when doing something is the way to go.

If you are reading a chapter entitled Guerrilla Warfare, you'll have to change the way you think about your dog. In order to learn how to do that, you'll need a set of rules to follow. I urge you to take them seriously and follow them religiously.

You will also need specific advice about all the common dog problems. An *alpha*betical list follows. It is extensive enough that you will probably be able to look up your dog's problem. But don't worry if your dog's particular problem hasn't made the hit list. Many dog problems have the same root causes and many corrective measures work with broad strokes, fixing, happily, even more than you intended.

Chapter Nine includes not only typical dog problems such as destructive chewing and aggression, but also those problems described in Chapter One as the hallmarks of adolescence. If you found your dog there, you will find the help you need here.

All of the behaviors discussed are likely to emerge or be exacerbated during adolescence, but not all at once and not all in every dog. Most of these problems should give you no more cause for alarm than pimples on a teenager. However, any dog problem emerging in adolescence should inspire a change in your behavior, a change in rules and lifestyle for your dog and the following of whatever suggestions match the particular problems your dog exhibits. Left to his own devices, your dog will probably *not* outgrow his problems. The vast numbers of dogs in shelters are testimony to that. You must take charge and teach him which behaviors are acceptable and which are not.

THE RULES OF WARFARE

NO DOGS ON THE FURNITURE   Yes, this includes your bed. Dogs sharing seating and sleeping surfaces will instantly treat you like a littermate and, a moment later, like a subordinate.

NO FREE TREATS   Give your dog his one or two meals a day and *no* treats until he deserves them—probably when he's forty! If you are training with treats, now is the time to stop. You will not win the respect of a teenager by popping cheese into his mouth.

USE THE LONG DOWN, ONE-HOUR LONG, ONCE A DAY It is a benign ritual which shows the dog who is in charge. It also can calm a wild dog.

MAKE SURE YOUR DOG GETS ONE HOUR OF CON-STRUCTIVE EXERCISE EVERY DAY Good options include playing with other dogs, getting a training lesson, long walks. Being tied to a tree in your yard does not count as one hour of exercise.

ALWAYS KEEP A BUCKLE COLLAR ON YOUR DOG WHEN YOU ARE HOME WITH HIM In this way, you can make a serious feeling correction should that be necessary. Trust me, it will be.

MAKE YOUR DOG WORK FOR PETTING Do not let your dog bully, manipulate or entice you into long petting sessions. Instead, if he comes and pesters you for attention, either ignore him or ask him to work for it—sit and stay, retrieve, do a trick, etc. Let him get into the habit of earning his rewards. An appreciative adolescent is preferable to an arrogant, overbearing one.

TAKE EVERY OPPORTUNITY YOU CAN TO INTEGRATE YOUR DOG'S TRAINING INTO YOUR LIFESTYLE   In other words, use it: Have him sit and stay for a moment before he gets his dinner, at the door before going out, at the mailbox, etc. Use the down-stay to keep him near you, yet well behaved, during meals. On each and every walk, let him free walk and relieve himself, then heel him on the way home. If he pulls to get into your house, pass your house several times so that he understands that you are the boss. Take him with you whenever you can—to the store, the bank, the dry cleaner, if you know dogs are allowed—but make him work as you go. For large dogs, try saddlebags and have him *really* work by helping you carry things.

MAKE SURE YOU CAN EASILY GET YOUR TROUBLE-MAKER'S ATTENTION   There are many ways to encourage your dog to form the positive habit of looking *to* you (rather than *at* you) for direction or approval. You should use them all.

- Put your dog on a sit-stay, correct him if he breaks and wait. Eventually, he will make the decision to look at you, to see what's going to happen next. Praise him when he does, release him from the stay and praise again when he comes to you.
- Teach your dog to respond to "Watch me" by looking up and into your eyes. Put him on a sit-stay, say, "Watch me," and, at the same moment, bring your hand from your side quickly (but not so quickly that your hand is quicker than his eye) to your eye. Praise him for looking into your eyes. As you practice, try to increase the time he will look. Your dog's expression should be friendly, attentive and curious. Your eyes should express a kind of friendly strength, not anger. Direct, angry eye contact is intensely threatening, or, in the case of an aggressive dog, intensely inflammatory. Never stare hard into a dog's eyes, unless he is your own dog, he is absolutely unaggressive and he has just done something horrendous. Never under any circumstances should you stare at a strange dog. That alone could provoke an attack. Staring is an act of aggression in dogs, just as it is in humans. Your own pet will learn the difference between friendly eye contact and what-did-you-do! eye contact. Surely, you can and should look into your dog's eyes. But you should know the power of eye contact and use it wisely.

Watch me! Good boy, Holden!

- When you are out on a walk with your dog, once or twice in a long walk, click your tongue, whistle, jingle keys, squeak a toy, imitate a bird, whine like a puppy or simply say your dog's name. When he turns to look questioningly into your eyes, praise him for doing so and let him continue on ahead. Don't badger.
- Practice getting your dog's attention when you are working him, particularly if he is frantic, anxious, inattentive, nervous or forgets you exist. His mood will improve greatly once his attention is on you—and so will his performance. First, you should have an absolutely clear picture of what you want from him at the moment, for example, attentive heeling. Next, project your goal to the dog by walking in one direction and turning sharply in the opposite direction when your dog's attention fades. Do not warn him you are turning. It's his job to watch you, to be attentive. Simply turn and walk quickly back the way you came, forcing a firm leash correction as the dog, continuing along unmindful in the opposite direction, comes to the end of the leash. If you have a Yorkie, modulate your correction. Anything bigger than a breadbox is unlikely to break from a quick, firm correction with a nylon slip collar. After a few such turns, your dog will be paying attention.

- Continue to heel with your dog, occasionally making a sound to get him to look at you. Praise him warmly when he looks and do a few turns if his attention drifts again.

The adolescent dog is notoriously inattentive. For safety's sake, you must work at getting his attention, despite distractions. If your dog has behavior problems, you must be able to get and hold his attention if you are going to have any success at teaching him a better mode of behavior. Without attention, there is no learning. Without eye contact, there really isn't attention. Of course, your dog need not heel with his eyes locked to yours. He should be able to look about and both absorb and enjoy the scenery. But he should not forget you're there. Once you can get his attention easily, you'll know that even when interested and distracted, he has saved a small portion in the corner of his mind just for you. Good enough! Now you are ready to deal with any problems your dog may have.

9

DEALING WITH YOUR DOG'S PROBLEMS

AGGRESSION — WILDNESS
AN *ALPHABETICAL* LIST

Aggression

How appropriate that the worst problem begins with an "a" and comes first, because if this is on your mind, nothing else counts until you resolve it. That is as it should be, because aggressiveness is dangerous and, if left unchecked, it only gets worse.

How will you know if your aggressive dog is a cheeky adolescent who needs to be trained, better exercised and put in his place or if your aggressive dog is a genetic disaster who is and will always be a menace to those he comes in contact with and should be put down? You may already know. *If you think your dog is an accident waiting to happen, he probably is.* If this is what you believe in your heart about your dog, the next logical step would be serious, difficult and permanent. If you feel your dog might be a lost cause and are considering euthanasia, I urge you not to make any decision without seeking professional help. You might indeed have to put your dog down. But the possibility also exists that someone with more knowledge and experience might be able to help you correct the problem and rehabilitate the dog.

Your first line of defense is always your dog's veterinarian. A fair amount of the aggression professional trainers see in dogs is caused by pain. Before you make any decision, have your veterinarian determine if your dog is in pain. If he is, he can't tell you about it and you may very well see no outward signs of it, other than his aggression. In many a dog's mind, if he hurts and you're there, it's your fault. A dysplastic dog may jump up to greet his owner and bite him instead when the jump causes the dog a shot of pain in his hips. Or you might simply reach your hand out to pet a dog, not knowing he's in pain. The dog, already on edge from pain, wants to be left alone. He bites your hand to chase you away.

Much can be done to alleviate pain, depending upon the cause, so do make careful notes about your dog's behavior; when it happens, what if anything seems to trigger the aggression, how it manifests itself and how long it lasts. Include weather conditions if your dog seems more aggressive, for example, on damp days. Bring the list with you when you take your dog to see the veterinarian. If your veterinarian rules out pain, he may very well be able to recommend the right person for your next step, an experienced professional dog trainer.

If your dog grabs hands and gloves, barks too much, nips but doesn't break the skin, try a group training class or a private obedience trainer in order to get his training right and tight and to learn how to properly correct your rude but basically normal, okay adolescent dog.

If your dog breaks the skin, scares you, seems or gets out of control, lunges at people when you walk him, backs you down, guards objects, growls when you approach him, if you can't take something away from him, if he's big and you aren't, hire a highly recommended professional trainer on a consultation basis to give you an assessment of your dog. Find out if his aggression can be stopped and if he will be a safe dog to keep. If not, you know what must be done. You cannot give him away or put him up for adoption. He must be euthanized. And while I believe in giving every dog a fair shake, and I absolutely think, in this case, a professional opinion is necessary, I do not believe in beating around the bush when a dog is dangerous to humans. I have been told so many times that so and so is "a perfectly good dog" except for his biting. A biting dog is *not* a perfectly good dog. He is much closer to being a perfectly bad dog.

Many owners of aggressive dogs and even many dog trainers working with aggressive dogs spend a lot of time and energy trying to classify aggression, most importantly, trying to figure out if they are dealing with dominance aggression or fear-based aggression. It may be, at the outset, perfectly obvious to you which type of customer your dog is—a pushy, confident dominant dog or a potential fear biter. The answer *may* be revealed in the dog's body language as well as in his behavior. The dominant dog tends to approach life with everything forward and up, eyes staring, tail up and out and slowly moving. He's always visible, too, demanding a treat, a game or some petting, rushing through the doorway ahead of you, landing on your bed before you get a chance to hop into it yourself. The fearful dog who shows aggression displays a mixed message. He may stare, too, but perhaps his ears are back or his tail is tucked. Even as he growls, something about him should telegraph his fear, perhaps his eyes. If you don't know which kind of aggressive dog you have, you may discover which kind as you work with him. But more important than classifying him is changing your behavior toward him and his toward you. And very much of what you will do, and *not do*, will be the same with either type.

No matter the source of the aggression, the first thing you will want to do is to get the dog to become the follower as you become the leader. You can start this simply when you walk your dog on-leash. (It would be foolhardy to do *any* work, indoors or out, without a leash when your dog tends to be aggressive.) Begin your walk and after a while, do an about turn and walk the other way.

And again, walk a while, and about turn. The dog, on-leash, must follow you. This is a good beginning. You are acting the leader, he the follower, even if it is sort of symbolic.

Again, no matter the source of the aggression, neither type of dog should be taken lightly. Neither should be challenged or cornered. Both types need training, too. The dominant dog needs rules and obedience to put him in his appropriate place in the family and to get him down a peg or two. The fearful dog needs training to build his confidence so that he knows what is expected of him and knows he can deliver it. Fearful dogs don't like surprises. Rules and order can help them cope.

Perhaps you can easily tell which type of aggression your dog is exhibiting, dominance based or fear based. If you can't, don't spend your time worrying about it when you could be spending it retraining your pet. More important than type is the severity of the aggression. In other words, will a firm no change your dog's behavior and will obedience class plus outdoor exercise make him safe to be around? Or are we dealing with a more difficult adversary, a dominant dog who will come at you harder each time his dominance is challenged as *eventually* it must be? And is the fearful dog a nervous, defensive dog who can be built up to feel confident and calm, or is he so damaged, of such poor genetic material that he simply cannot let go of his ghosts? These are the important questions, and also, can you answer them by yourself or do you need help?

While you are in the process of finding out how serious your dog's aggression is, pay very careful attention to the rules in the previous chapter. You do not want this dog on your bed. You do not want to be fawning over this dog, telling him with each treat and each stroke on his fur that he is alpha and you worship him. You can love him, even if he is a bad egg. But you must not act like a littermate or subordinate to him. It will only encourage him to be more aggressive.

If your dog's aggression scares you, you should be working only with an experienced trainer. If you work without help and even accidentally challenge your dog, he will probably come at you, frighten you and make you back down. Each experience like this, where the dog *wins*, makes him a stronger adversary, a more dangerous dog.

Don't feel bad if you are scared. Trainers get scared, too. The difference is that we have learned how to make the fear work for us, to move through it, as it were, and correct the dog. We have also learned, sometimes by doing it wrong and getting bitten, many techniques to work effectively yet safely. Most of all, we have greater experience reading dogs and can usually (this is an art, not a science) tell the difference between a spoiled brat and a menace.

If your dog is a male and the onset of his aggression is recent, consider neutering him. Neutering may not solve the problem entirely, but it *may* (no guarantees) tone him down, perhaps just enough for you to be able to work successfully with him. If he is aggressive, neutering is a good decision anyway because he surely should not be bred. The last thing this world needs is more aggressive dogs. Neutering will also stop much of the aggression *toward* him by other male dogs. If he is getting into spats with other males and *not* starting the fights, neutering can improve his lot. Neutered, he will no longer smell like a threat to other males. If he is not the innocent mark but the instigator of fights, neutering can remove some of his feelings of tension and rivalry with other males. If his fighting has not become habitual or learned behavior and if you are able to act very soon after the onset of his dog aggression, he may, in time, become benign enough to play with other males.

While not a panacea, neutering can be an important part of the solution to dog aggression. Many dogs seem calmer after neutering, less tightly wired and thus less on the lookout for a fight. Neutered dogs do not become less playful, nor do they become fat if they are appropriately fed and exercised.

When working with an aggressive dog, less is more. Work for short periods of time, taking all necessary precautions. If you push, push, push, your dog will eventually explode.

Instead, watch for signs of tension, the precursor to biting in most cases. When the dog gets tense, do not try to control him further. Get him outside and get him moving. The movement alone will help release his tension. Then, by working on heeling and recalls, you can begin to slowly inculcate the habit of following, first literally and then figuratively. As your dog follows you, by heeling, by coming, he is also following your bidding. He is obeying you. This means you are winning his respect. Over time, you will be able to do more with him, to get more from him, but only if you work slowly and carefully, not in a provocative, inflammatory way.

Should the dog act aggressive toward you, try not to back down. That would make him a stronger, more confident aggressor. This is why it helps to work with a trainer. But, suppose despite all precautions, one day your dog does lunge, growl or snap at you during a training session. Instead of pressing forward and getting bitten, adopt an attitude that says, "Oh, who cares about that!" Instead of addressing the growl, turn away, command, "Heel," and walk *quickly* in another direction, neither turning to see if your dog is following or stopping to wait for him to make up his mind. He's on-leash. He has to come or get corrected. Your failure to be bullied will have him nonplussed. This is a much safer way of winning your point than going nose to nose with a scary, aggressive dog. Heel quickly, make lots of turns and keep him working and moving. Get a brief sit-stay, not long enough to give him time to start thinking. Break the stay, praise your dog and quit for the day. When you get back home, don't forget to start breathing again.

In all probability, you already know just when your aggressive dog is dangerous. You may not know the best way to retrain him. You may indeed need help. But you do know what situations tend to make him tense, what events make him on edge. You even know what creates those awful moments when he's like a grenade with the pin pulled. So take care of yourself. Some trainer friends of mine use Binaca breath spray, aimed into the dog's mouth at precisely the moment of an aggressive snarl. Sometimes plain water will do. I once reached behind me into a client's sink and tossed a full pot of cold water into the face of her dog as he came at me. It stopped him—cold. When my heartbeat came back to normal, I even helped my client clean up the kitchen. Some dogs back off from a plant mister, the water laced with white vinegar. Some back off if you aim a shot of Real Lemon into their open mouths. These measures are all meant for defense only, for those times when you didn't see the tension or the aggression building, those times when the dog just turns mean, seemingly out of the blue.

You also know by now just how your aggressive dog expresses

himself. Does he hover over a toy, a rag or a bone growling and slathering? If he guards an object, try getting rid of it. If he growls every time he gets a bone or rawhide to chew, do not give him bones or rawhide. If these measures don't help, if he just keeps finding other things to guard, hire a trainer.

If your object-guarding *he* is a *she* and she is object guarding during a false pregnancy, let her ride it out. However, if she has repeated false pregnancies, you should seriously consider having her spayed.

What if your dog guards his food? You can't not feed him. Although it was necessary for survival in the wild, your pet dog does not need to guard his food. If your dog growls over his food bowl, he does not respect you. He would never try to protect his food from someone he knew was higher ranked than he. Before you do anything direct about his food guarding, go back to Chapter Two and work again on winning his respect. Otherwise you will get nowhere.

Once your dog starts looking to you for direction and obeys your commands but he still growls over his food, do not feed him unless his leash is on. Always use a leash when asking him to do *anything*, even indoors, just in case. Should he growl at your presence in the room, pick up the leash, bellow "No" and give one sideways tug on the leash. Should your dog continue to growl, remove him from his food (he's on-leash, isn't he?) and remove the food until his next regularly scheduled meal.

In addition, when you catch your dog in a more pleasant mood, after he has eaten more than half of his dinner, call him to you, just a foot or so away from his dish, ask him to sit and place a wondrously delicious goody in his bowl, telling him okay as soon as you stand up again. Then let him finish his meal in peace. Try this no more than twice a week.

This combination of correcting growling and teaching your dog that your presence around his bowl is to his benefit should stop the food guarding *if* you have really won your dog's respect. If you cannot get him to stop guarding food, since this is a problem of aggression, you probably will need the help of a professional dog trainer.

Make *sure* the aggressive dog is getting sufficient outdoor exercise. What is sufficient? Make him *tired*. Do not (I certainly repeat myself when it's important, don't I?), do not let the dog sleep on your bed. Do not fawn over the dog, petting him whenever he asks for affection. Think seriously about neutering. Check with your veterinarian about possible medical causes of the aggression. If you need it, and you probably do, seek professional advice and professional help. If you try everything humanly possible and you fail to rehabilitate your dog, do not pass the problem on to someone else.

Barking

Barking, or too much barking, may not seem to be one of the major dog problems unless you're living with it. If you live in an apartment, it can earn you the wrath of your neighbors and maybe an eviction notice. But even if you live in the woods, it can give you a royal headache.

Some dogs are simply noisier than others. While you cannot completely silence any dog, nor should you want to, you can do two helpful things with the noisy dog. You can give your dog several reasonable outlets for his voice by teaching him to bark on command and then teaching him some tricks and games where he is *supposed* to use his voice. Once this is accomplished, you can use the term *enough* to quiet him when he gets carried away with the melodious sound of his own bark.

In order to teach your dog to bark on command, choose a word and stick to it. I use speak but I also use a hand signal: two fingers snapping up and down quickly like a talking mouth. The hand signal gives you flexibility in speaking tricks and has a bonus that has to do with safety.

Observe your noisy dog and see what makes him bark. Make a list—and then use it. You can actually teach barking on command with a set up. For example, if your dog barks when the doorbell rings, ask a friend to ring your bell as you stay at your dog's side and enthusiastically tell him, "Speak, good dog, speak!" Most dogs will learn to bark on command within a week. Many will do it in a day or two if you start them by barking yourself.

Once your dog will bark on your signal, he is no longer simply responding to outdoor noises or his desire to manipulate you into a game. Now he is responding to a command. He is aware of you.

He is obeying you. He is just where you want him. Now, after a bark or two, tell him, "Enough." If your tone won't silence him, slip your hand into his collar, give one yank sideways and repeat your command, enough. Praise warmly for compliance.

What shall you do when your dog barks at the door? Praise him for alerting you, tell him enough, ask him to sit and praise him again. When you open your door, he should be sitting at your side, alert, but no longer barking.

Now add other legitimate uses of his voice. You can ask him to speak for a cookie, to go out, for his dinner, to do anything, as long as it's at your request. You can have him add numbers, asking him, "How much is two and two?" and starting him with, you guessed it, the hand signal. Of course, you'll have to help him to get the right answer. After he has barked four times, simply tell him, "Good dog." This will stop the barking and make your dog look smart indeed. (If you want him to look like a genius, ask him to bark the square root of sixteen instead of two plus two!) Your dog will love to do barking tricks because of the chance to use his voice without getting yelled at and because of the praise he'll get for each "right answer."

Suppose you've done all this work and one night you hear a funny sound outside your door or window, someone lurking, someone looking for a way in. If you say, "Speak, speak," what good would it do? Who would be afraid of your trick dog? But

Of course, you'll have to help him get the right answer.

suppose you use your hand signal. Then you can say anything you like—"Watch him! Who's there? Watch him. Good dog!" and so on. So your extra work to quiet down a noisy dog can offer a little protection in our iffy world. Even if you just get some peace and quiet, the work is worth it.

Bossy, Manipulative, Always Testing

The bossy, manipulative dog needs training, and once that is accomplished, he needs little tune-ups several times a week. Even a trained adolescent dog will forget himself every now and then. In truth, he'll forget himself more now than then! So once he has learned the basic commands, make sure you use them daily. You can use some indoors, requiring him to sit and stay while you prepare his food or put his collar and leash on. If he plays little games when you try to put his collar on, make sure he wears a buckle collar indoors when you are home. You can fasten the buckle collar on him before you take off the slip collar, and vice versa, so that you have something to hold when he's trying to move his head away and keep control.

Don't play with this brat every time he dumps a ball in your lap. Ignore him, or make him work for what he wants. Do a little indoor tune-up before a game—a sit-stay, a recall, a five-minute down-stay. Play ball as his reward for obedience.

Use long downs when he's too *up*, too cheeky, too loud, too anything. And if you've really had it, take a time-out by crating him for half an hour.

The bossy dog will want to run things. The more temptation around, the more motivated he'll be to challenge you. So when you take him to visit friends with dogs, make sure you work the dogs together—a group sit-stay, a group down-stay—as part of their time together. The strong message of leadership you present by doing this will not only garner you better behavior from your dog, it will also help prevent conflicts among the dogs.

Doing all of the above will get you exactly nowhere if your exuberant teen is not getting enough exercise. Running around out of doors, good, constructive, active games with you or with some dog friends, an outdoor obedience tune-up that includes lots of fast heeling, swimming, jogging, climbing flights of stairs, retrieving—these activities will make your adolescent dog more mellow, more tractable, and, thank you God, tired. Every dog needs a positive outlet for his energy. None need it more than adolescent dogs. So if your dog is constantly testing, manipulative and bossy, tighten up his responses to obedience commands, enroll him in a group class so that he learns to obey even with other dogs around, play lots of active games with him, do not give in everytime he wants something and make sure he is getting at least a full hour of constructive activity every day.

Brute Force

You just have to face it, the adolescent dog does not know his own strength. More than that, his self-control is poor. Add to that his overwhelming enthusiasm, his joie de vivre, his clumsiness and you have a couple of years of black and blue marks to look forward to. Of course, if your adolescent is a delicate toy, a graceful sight hound, a little mixed-breed dog, you won't have a problem worth discussing. On the other bruised hand, if your dog is a big, strong klutz like most of the teenagers my little tank plays with, expect to be bumped into, crushed, pulled and pushed—all with the best intentions. Even after adolescence, big dogs can hurt you accidentally. When you play with them or when they are running around, you're going to get your toes stomped and your body bashed. That's just the way it is.

Unlike me, try to be aware when damage is almost guaranteed. One day, in the dog run, I foolishly stood instead of sitting on one of the benches that line the fence. On top of that, I didn't have eyes behind my head, silly me. At one point I was hit full tilt by a joyous group of five or six half-grown lunatic dogs who were happily racing from one end of the run to the other and back again and having the time of their lives. I should have been more alert, but, no big deal. Bruises heal and I lived to tell the tale.

Be prepared for the bump, the crush, the smash and, most of all, the sudden hard pull on the leash when your teen spots another dog. That's just about all the damage control you can do and still let your dog be a dog and have a wonderful time.

Coprophagy

If you don't know how to pronounce coprophagy, don't give it a thought. You won't want to talk about it, so you won't have to know how to say it. Coprophagy refers to the habit some dogs have of eating feces, theirs or someone else's. This is almost always considered a behavior problem, but it isn't always. If your dog indulges himself in this way, examine the following possible causes: digestive problems, including pancreatic insufficiency and malabsorption, boredom, lack of exercise, too much opportunity, severe punishment for housebreaking accidents.

The first possibility, digestive problems, should be discussed with your veterinarian. He or she may want to test the dog's stool to see how well he is digesting his food. He may suggest medication or a change of diet. Where this problem exists, The Merck Veterinary Manual suggests feeding twice a day, using a high-protein, low-carbohydrate feed with a little vegetable oil added. Your own veterinarian may have additional helpful suggestions.

If your dog is paper trained and left alone a lot or if he is in the run or yard all day long, he may be eating stools because they are available and he is bored. In this case, you can attack the problem from two sides. First, enroll your dog in obedience class and begin to train him and take him places with you. In other words, address his mind and give him adventures. At the same time, don't clean up all the stools, but instead sprinkle or spray something nasty-tasting on them, Bitter Apple or chili powder. This may convince your dog to change his habits. You can also see what happens if you clean up more often, thus removing temptation. While you're at it, try giving your dog a two-week moratorium on excrement eating by walking him someplace other than his yard, distracting him with a favorite toy immediately after he relieves himself and then scooping. This may break the habit. If during this time, you find times you can't walk him, late at night or in the rain, use a muzzle when you let him out into the yard to prevent him from continuing this offensive habit.

If you are storming at your dog when he has housebreaking accidents, you should tone down your corrections and try prevention plus praise for appropriate behavior. But be warned that this habit is difficult to cure. For whatever reason, dogs can be rather persistent about it. Remember, too, mother dogs clean up after their pups by ingesting their feces. Coprophagy is more of a problem for *us* than for dogs. They don't seem to mind it at all.

Crazy Behavior

Many people write to ask my advice about their dogs. This case was particularly interesting because the dog's behavior seemed so puzzling at first.

> Dear Carol,
> I have a really weird problem with my Wire Fox Terrier. Every time the front doorbell rings, Roland runs to the door, barking like crazy. If I let the person in, Roland grabs ankles or pants, pulling, growling and carrying on like a lunatic.
>
> Lest you think he's protecting the house, let me tell you the strangest part. When someone comes to the back door, Roland doesn't budge off the couch. At most, he might walk over sleepily to see who's there. I can't understand this behavior and, more important, I don't know what to do about it. Can you help?

Here is my advice:

Roland believes it is his job to protect the front door. He will not give up this behavior until you convince him that it is not your wish that he bark at and attack your visitors. In order to do this, create the situation that triggers the unwanted behavior when you are in control. In other words, pay a few brave teenagers the going rate for bell ringing, have them come at an appointed time and ring your doorbell. Have Roland on-leash and walk him to the door. When he starts to bark, jerk and release with your leash, saying, "Enough," in a firm tone. Then command your dog to sit and stay. Keeping good control of dog and leash, open the door and instruct the "visitor" to either wait or come in, depending upon the control you have over Roland. As you work, correct all signs of aggression.

Once you have corrected Roland a few times with a few different visitors, you should be able to get a quick sit-stay and be able to allow people to enter unharmed. Proceed slowly and with caution.

This will solve your problem. You should also consider what Roland needs.

Alertness and activity are the hallmarks of the Fox Terrier. Given nothing constructive to do, an alert and clever mind will make work for itself. Most dogs do not get enough exercise. Here, you are lucky to have a Fox Terrier. Though your dog needs outdoor exercise, too, he can do some of his running about indoors. Obviously, Roland needs encouragement in this area. He has too much available energy for doing mischief.

You might try giving Roland a rubber ball, a crunched-up foil ball, and a large, hard ball he can push around. With the rubber and foil balls, see if you can get him to chase the ball and bring it back. Next, see if you can get Roland to drop the ball into your shoe. The more his smart, little brain gets to work along with his body, the better.

Of course, I'm assuming Roland knows the basic commands. But are they tight? If not, work on them, one at a time, until you get a good response.

Fox Terriers are fabulous at tricks and having one that doesn't know a few dignified tricks is probably against the law someplace. You can teach any dog to jump when you're out of doors by using low obstacles, decorative fences, railroad ties, a low stone wall. Once Roland is hooked on jumping, you can set up a temporary jump indoors with a broomstick. Now you can toss the ball over the jump and have him hop over, get the ball, hop back and put the ball in your shoe. You can't get much more dignified than that.

As to why Roland chooses to protect the front door and not the back, who knows? Perhaps he learned this accidentally by "chasing away" the postman everyday. Perhaps the back door is used only by family and his crazy behavior really has a very logical origin. The whole scenario might have made sense at some point early on. Then when it became a push-button reaction, it lost its original meaning. Perhaps Roland's crazy habit is a combination of factors—more smarts and energy than he was using constructively, the irritating sound of the front doorbell, the "accident" of certain visitors leaving after he had barked, your failure to communicate clearly that his behavior was unwanted and perhaps some genetic input that makes old Roland a bit more jumpy than he should be.

As our lives become more complicated, so do our dogs' lives. I have seen cases far more peculiar than Roland's.

Take the case of the Borzoi who turned on the kitchen faucet every time his owner left him alone. (No, his water bowl wasn't empty.) Perhaps he was lonely and associated the sound of the running water with his owner's presence at home. It's hard to tell how these things get started. Often you miss the very early clues and by the time you see the weird habit, you might be months away from what started it. You might not even remember the event.

Occasionally you hear that a dog will let people into the house, but not out. Some Shelties I knew of would get fed by a neighbor. They'd let him in, but when he tried to leave, the dogs would bite him. This is a case of nervous dogs who don't like change. Okay, they say, we let you in. We put up with that. But no way are we letting you out. Of course, if the dogs are a bit nervous, they're more likely to bite when your back is turned and you are "retreating." It gets their courage up.

Some of the nuttiest behavior I've seen has to do with object guarding. Dogs will guard the oddest things, an old sock, a dish towel, a half of a toy. In these situations, the histories may be complex. The reasons why a dog does these things may have to do with genetics as well as owner behavior, owner mistakes. But the first thing to do is always the same. Have someone take the dog out for a long walk. While he's out, get rid of what he guards—forever.

To generalize about crazy behavior, I'd say, first, stop the behavior mechanically. Do not allow the dog to continue doing the crazy thing. Allowing the behavior approves of the behavior. Second, assume that your dog needs more exercise. The more energy he uses up constructively, the less he'll have to be nuts with. Third, tighten the training. Get eye contact, too. Fourth, before getting into any specifics about why he does what he does, play some games with him every day, active, wholesome games, played outdoors whenever possible.

What makes our dogs crazy? Who knows? We live in a crazy world.

Destructiveness and Stealing

Here's a "case" that started with the arrival of an oversized manila envelope with the return address of a law firm on it. Inside, there was a copy of one of my own books, chewed and torn. An entire chapter had been wrenched from the binding and partially shredded, then replaced where it belonged in the book. The following letter was enclosed:

> Dear Carol:
> I thought you would appreciate the irony of this situation. I purchased your book because my seven-month-old Samoyed puppy, Sonoma, loves to steal objects from around the apartment. One day, she went into my briefcase and ran off with *Dog Problems* and ate the chapter on "Larceny—Petty and Grand" before I had a chance to read it. Enclosed is the evidence. Please help.

I called to get more details. Sonoma would steal to get attention, causing Ed and his girlfriend, Vicki, to chase her through the apartment trying to retrieve whatever treasure she had taken. There was a chronic housebreaking problem, too. I was surprised to learn that the dog got sufficient exercise—lack of same is so common where there are dog problems—and unsurprised to hear that she did not come reliably when called but would extend her time in the park by acting deaf or playing a game of keepaway. There had been some earlier training—sit, down, stay, heel. Despite her rowdy behavior, the dog was adored. I decided to take the case.

THE CONSULTATION

With her white coat and friendly Spitz smile, teenage Sonoma was the picture of a perfect angel, until you looked at her dancing dark eyes. There it was clear—Sonoma rules. Like so many dogs who *know* they are alpha, she makes her own fun.

In order to see how dog and owner related, I asked Ed to show me Sonoma's sit-stay. He put her on command in the middle of the living room, dropped her leash and returned to his chair at the table where Vicki and I were waiting and watching. As soon as he sat, Sonoma broke. Ed got up, went back to Sonoma, picked up the leash, put the dog on a sit-stay, dropped the leash and returned to his chair. As soon as he sat, Sonoma broke again. Each time the procedure was repeated, Ed performed the identical steps, never getting annoyed, never escalating his "correction."

When Vicki worked Sonoma, the dog broke even more quickly. But in addition to dropping the leash and walking away, a step this dog was clearly not ready for, Vicki's chair was on the opposite side of the table from the dog. She not only became smaller and thus less alpha when she sat down, she all but disappeared. I asked her to try again, but this time to stay six feet from the dog, holding the leash. Sonoma did not break.

With Sonoma on a long down, a suggested daily practice from now on, we discussed the issue of alpha and how the various body language clues Ed and Vicki gave the dog undermined their leadership. I suggested they work away from the dog in stages, first holding the leash, next standing nearby with the leash dropped, finally sitting. I told them not to give any verbal commands after the first break. Certainly Sonoma was smart enough to know she broke a sit and did not have to be told to sit again. A leash correction, done quickly and with authority, would be sufficient.

Sonoma's favorite game, larceny, was easy to control. I suggested Ed and Vicki tie a long string to her collar when they were at home and when Sonoma stole, teased and took off, to hold their ground and call her. When she didn't come, they were to tug the string, praise her (but not warmly) for coming and, by command, have her drop the object. If she failed to release the object, they were to take it, opening her mouth by clasping her muzzle from above, as this procedure works by spoiling the fun of the game. I warned them never to tug the object from her mouth as that would teach her to hold on tighter and increase the fun of the game for her.

The trickiest problem was the housebreaking and here I decided that a big change and a big risk were in order. The dog was not only barking and urinating in her crate, but urinating many times a day on paper that was left down for her in the living room. Since the dog was urinating so excessively, I asked if they had discussed this with their veterinarian and was told that there was no medical problem. I suggested the removal of the crate and all paper, and gradually cutting the walks to four and finally three per day. I thought the time was right for elevating expectations of Sonoma without, of course, being totally foolhardy. The dog was to be confined at night in the bedroom. Submissive urination was to be ignored. Water was to be removed after dinner. Finally, during the short periods of time when no one was home, Sonoma would be confined in the kitchen with a gate, a system they had already used successfully.

During subsequent phone consultations, I learned that larceny was no longer a problem. The string had done the trick. Sonoma's response to the daily long down-stays was better but not perfect. One day she'd lie down immediately. The next day she'd be a feisty adolescent, testing and pushing to try to get her way. But even on her bad days, she'd only fight for a minute and then stay.

Sonoma stayed clean and dry all night. She was better during the day, but not all better. There were still occasional accidents and the submissive urination persisted.

While there are still problems, Sonoma has proven herself willing to relearn and capable of more responsibility. Spitz breeds usually need more training time than Sporting or Working dogs. They are not nearly as interested in pleasing their owners as they are in pleasing themselves. All in all, I was happy with the progress after one session, but could see that more work was needed. I urged Ed and Vicki to take Sonoma to dog obedience class, which would give them ten weeks of support in learning how to take charge and handle their pet in a loving yet firm way.

With commitment from her owners and time to grow up, even a tough to train dog with the word *no* in her name should eventually learn to be an obedient and satisfying pet.

Your destructive dog should not have run of the house. Even a well-trained, well-exercised adolescent can destroy its owner's possessions, so tightening training and giving your dog enough exercise are essential, but so is prevention. When you have a puppy or an adolescent dog, it is wise to move valuables out of reach. Of course, you can't put your couch away for the duration. But perhaps the dog need not have access to the living room. In any case, having a dog should make you a little neater, offering him less to rip up when the chew mood strikes.

If your dog can be crated when you go out, this is ideal in terms of safeguarding your possessions. However, if you are gone all day, it is not ideal for your dog. It's just not fair to keep a grown or half-grown dog confined in a crate all day.

Perhaps you have a room that can be pretty much dogproofed, the kitchen, for example. Always work your dog a little before you leave to remind him to respect you and to make him feel secure. Exercise also helps a lot. Tired out, he'll chew a toy for a few minutes and then go to sleep. Leaving the radio on helps some dogs feel they are not so terribly alone. This is important because one of the major causes of chewing is anxiety. Even humans try to relieve anxiety orally, chewing gum, smoking, drinking, noshing. So it shouldn't be difficult to understand that a dog, a pack animal never designed to find himself alone for hours on end, would feel anxious when left alone all day, particularly when he is young and foolish.

In cities, some working people hire a dog walker to come during the day and take their dog out for exercise. For those who can afford to do this, it's a great solution. It is wonderful for the dog to have this outdoor break during the day. It also takes the pressure off the owner to rush right home immediately after work. It can help save the furniture, too.

If you want another pet, the company might help your young dog not feel lonesome. But since he won't take care of the other pet, another dog or a cat, and he won't pay the veterinary bills, this has to be something you want to do.

Be sure your dog has a supply of things to chew. You can rotate toys and chew things, leaving three or four out and putting the others away, then changing the set every few days to keep old toys exciting. Also try saving a favorite type of chew toy for when you leave, as a sort of good news–bad news deal.

Don't fuss when you go. A pat on the head and a simple, "Be good," will do. And don't fuss when you return. Keep your comings and goings low key and matter of fact. That, too, will help keep your dog calm so that he is less likely to chew.

But what happens if, despite everything you do, he does chew? If you see your dog chomping on your Gucci shoes or even on a favorite old pair of sweat socks, tell him, "No, out," take the item and put it away. Next, as fast as you can, offer something legitimate in its place and, as he takes it, tell him, "Good boy." Even if you were about to throw out the sweat socks, don't give them to your dog to chew. He can't tell the difference between your junk and your best duds. Don't invite trouble and don't assume he's incredibly more perceptive than he is.

Suppose you're home and the dog does his handiwork in another room. You walk in and catch him in the act of eating your bedspread or the molding. Grasp his collar, give it a shake (side to side), telling him, "No, shame!" (while you'll want to vent a lot, particularly if it's an expensive bedspread, be firm and keep your cool), shove the thing he chewed at his face, tell him, "Bad dog," and give yourself a time-out by crating him. That way you'll have time to forgive him before you have to deal with him again.

Suppose you come home from work and, God forbid, find the couch pillow chewed. Even though you'll want to, don't kill the dog. Don't take him out to the park and when he's not looking, run away. Instead, count to five, take a breath, and *act* angry. Your real rage has no place in dog training. It can cause you to scare or hurt your dog. You may have been told that you cannot correct your dog when you don't catch him in the act. But most adolescent dogs are already smart enough not to chew in front of you. Furthermore, it is when you leave them alone that they become anxious and chew. So how can you catch them in the act? If the dog has left "evidence," a partially chewed pillow for example, you can use the evidence to "remind" him of what he did and you can correct him. Where there is no evidence, for example, your dog stole and ate the defrosting roast, you cannot remind the dog of what he did and therefore you cannot correct him. So when you come home to the torn gloves or couch pillow, take your dog by his collar, lead him to the scene of his crime, "find" the destroyed object, inhale deeply and audibly to express your shock at his behavior and, holding his collar so that he cannot flee, shove the thing he chewed in the direction of his face and reprimand him angrily. Afterward, crate him and ignore him for one hour. He will *not* sit in the crate ruing his behavior. But *you* need the time out to calm down and figure out how you will afford to fix or replace the chewed-up item. When you finish doing that, do one more thing. Ask yourself the following questions:

Is my energetic adolescent dog getting enough exercise?

Does my dog *really* respect me? (Hint: Does he stay when you ask him to?)

Am I giving my dog too much freedom and am I leaving too many tempting things around while he is still young and untrustworthy?

Prevention is always easier and more pleasant than correction for both owners and dogs. The more a dog respects you, the less

Am I giving my dog too much freedom?

likely he is to chew your possessions. One of your best protections against destructive chewing is—oh, no, she's going to say it again—exercise. A pent-up dog has to put his energy into *something*. And finally, know that no one ever raised a puppy to adulthood without losing some possessions. Nobody's *that* careful.

Fearfulness and Shyness

Case histories are valuble because they demonstrate how theory is applied with an individual. This case started, as many do, with a letter:

> Dear Ms. Benjamin,
> Currently I own four Golden Retrievers. Two were purchased and two were obtained through my work with a rescue program. In joining the program, I told the organizers that I would take dogs who might be difficult to place. My first dog that I adopted is a ten-year-old who is well adjusted, healthy and lively. It seems that her family just got tired of her. My newest secondhand dog, Abby, is a nine-month-old who was neglected and abused.
> I accepted Abby when she was eight months old. She had been kept continually crated with her sister for the previous six months. The bit of human attention she received was abusive. Physically she was in mediocre condition. Emotionally she was tattered.

Abby is now in good physical condition. Emotionally she has improved considerably but I am concerned that I do not know enough to ensure that she will have the best possible recovery. At first Abby was afraid of everything conceivable—her food bowl, a sneeze, the wind, the television, toys, people and a lifetime full of other things. At this point she has fewer fears but the intensity of the remaining fears is growing stronger. She initially ran from everything and would hide for hours if something frightened her. Now she is barking and growling (but still cowering) in response to her biggest fear—men.

I need direction. I have begun informal obedience training. My initial attempts ended up with her vomiting. I try to be upbeat and encouraging with her. She is intelligent, loving and beautiful. I want her to work through these problems. My biggest concern is that the newest development, growling and barking, is a sign that she may become a dog who bites out of fear. Can you help me?

My first view of Abby was of her cowering in a corner in the lobby of my building. She seemed to be trying to go through the wall to escape. As Terry and I went over the details of Abby's history, several men came and went. Abby did not bark or growl. Instead, she appeared to almost die of fright, trembling and averting her eyes.

I explained to Terry that obedience training, particularly the sit-stay and heeling, would be the tools we would use to get Abby through. Once she had a formula to follow, a way to behave, she'd be better able to cope. Outside, we had no trouble finding passing men, but at first it was nearly impossible to get Abby to sit and stay. If she stayed, she would nearly collapse, her belly touching the sidewalk. When walking around she would stay near Terry unless something frightened her, a stranger, particularly a male stranger, a baby carriage, a truck, someone carrying a package, a noise, in which case she would try to flee. But we persevered and finally got the dog to hold a sit-stay while men passed by.

On one of our stays, a young man carrying a box, double fear, stopped to ask what we were doing. Most New Yorkers truly are friendly people. We explained and in a burst of nerve, I asked if he'd help us by taking one step closer, nowhere near enough to be bitten. Abby held her stay and was warmly praised. In addition, the experience of watching us chat amiably with the young man was excellent for her.

After working on quiet streets, we then alternated between a busy street and more quiet side streets, to push and let up. This is a formula I find very helpful with shy dogs. After an hour or so, the sit-stay was working and to our joy, Abby not only sat *up*, rather than slinking, but began to sniff the air with interest as men passed by.

I explained to Terry that she would have to take the dog to the business section of her New Jersey town, as often as possible, to continue the work we had only begun. I also instructed her never to let Abby act out her fear by running and hiding under furniture, slinking, etc., all of which she had been allowing. Terry, understandably, was afraid to *correct* Abby's fear. But by using a sit-stay in a fear-provoking situation, she could correct Abby if she bolted because she would also be breaking the stay command.

A shy or fearful dog should also be praised royally for trying anything new, no matter how trivial. In fact, I told Terry to allow Abby access to things that bothered her and to praise her for sniffing. For example, to place an umbrella, closed, on the floor and leave it there for the dog to investigate. The same with a package, a hat, a new toy. Eventually the dog would become blasé about new things.

Next, we started on the heel, switching from a flat collar to a slip collar. In doing this, we upped our expectations of the dog dramatically and because we had done the groundwork with the sit-stay, because we had praised every minute effort on the dog's part, because we had not allowed her to act out any spooky behavior, in other words, because we had made appropriate demands and appreciated effort, the dog did not disappoint us. In no time, Abby was heeling. Now when something spooked her, you could see her thought process in her body language. She showed fear briefly, then continued working.

At two o'clock, Abby had looked freaky. At three forty-five, she was working like a normal dog. But there was lots of work ahead. I explained that this was only a beginning and that all would be lost if Terry didn't continue the pattern we had begun. I asked her to continue to expose the dog to passing men and take weeks of gradual closer exposure before attempting to have her handled by a gentle, willing man. But I could see the disappointment in Terry's eyes.

I asked my husband, Steve, to join us and to stand a few feet from Abby but not to look at her. In fact, I asked him to keep the weight of his attention from her and be very un-alpha. Being a dog trainer's husband, he understood perfectly, and a moment later was standing next to Abby, who was totally calm. "Lower your hand, honey," I said, and Terry and I watched while Steve stroked Abby's broad, golden head as she leaned toward him.

No abused dog could have a more caring, willing owner. Given this, and the responsiveness of the canine spirit, the prognosis for this beautiful dog is excellent.

Your adolescent dog may be bold as brass today, but he or she could change in an hour or in a week from now. Just as your dog experienced a fear period at about the age of eight weeks, he may experience another longer one in adolescence. Often he will develop a specific fear, suddenly cowering when he sees children, hears loud noises, is approached by other dogs. He may have been totally comfortable with all those things in prior months. Nonetheless, the sudden, strong fears that can occur in adolescence should be taken seriously if they are not to remain permanent.

I have seen cases where a dog hooks his fear onto one person, a member of the family he may not have seen in a while who happens to show up during the fear period, or a type of dog, perhaps shaggy ones. If this happens, it is important to use the dog's obedience training to give him the formula for his behavior, things he has done before that caused him no harm. For example, if the dog is afraid of children, start out by requesting a sit-stay whenever you see a child approaching on the street. The dog need not socialize with the child, indeed, most kids will just be passing by, but he cannot break his stay and act out his fear by hiding, running away or cowering behind you. Understand that the fear is quite real, but if you work patiently with your dog, he can emerge on the other side of it in good shape.

After you have gotten your dog to stay when children pass him on the street, you may see a return of interest. He may, as Abby did, sniff the air as they pass. Praise him warmly whenever he shows benign interest or curiosity. This is a good sign.

The next step, and this may be weeks or months after the onset of the fear, is to ask very nice, quiet children to call him over. If he can make the approach, it will be easier for him. But he may still be afraid to do that. If the dog is gentle and never aggressive, you can invite the child to approach the dog while the dog is on his sit-stay. Watch the dog closely. If he gets very tense, ask the child not to come closer. A slight approach is better than an all-out one, particularly if the dog is tense.

As you work, stand behind your dog while he does his sit-stay, holding your feet with the toes out around his body in Charlie Chaplin fashion, thus bracing the dog and giving him security. You can also brace him with his collar by slipping your hand into it and holding him firm. Of course, when you do this, he cannot get away. More important, he will feel that you are right there, supporting him.

Make these sessions brief, praise your dog for every moment he faces his fear, and pay careful attention to his mood. There are times during the adolescent fear period when you will not be able to get him near what he fears. But it is important that he obey his command and that he is praised when he shows interest. Working in this way, you should be able to get him over his fear, but it does take time.

Your dog may have momentary fears of strange objects. These fears are much easier to deal with than fear of people or other dogs. First, teach your dog the fun command *smell it*. Dogs use their noses the way humans use their eyesight, so your dog will smell anything you show him. Show him a cookie, a pen, a tissue, a wallet, a glove, a leaf, a can, an apple, a sock, a book, etc., and say, "Smell it." You will see his nose working. Praise him. In no time flat, he'll know this new command. Later on, you can use it in games, but for now our interest is in using it when he has a sudden fear of an item he can't identify.

You are walking down the street and your dog sees an over-turned trash can. He balks. He tries to run. Or he goes belly down and shakes. He will not walk past it. Holding the end of the leash so that your dog does not bolt, walk nearer the can, pat it with your hand, and encourage him closer, saying, "Smell it, good dog, smell it." Your dog will slowly approach the can, sniff it and quickly get very bold. By smelling the trash can, he will know it is inanimate and harmless. So when he shows fear over an open umbrella set out to dry, a baby carriage or bicycle, a box, a rustling

Your dog will smell anything *you show him.*

The more you socialize your dog throughout his life, the less likely it is you'll end up with a timid, shy or fearful pet.

paper bag, tap it, tell him, "Smell it" and watch him become his old, bold self in no time. He will probably be so pleased with himself, he'll start sneezing.

A fear that arises during the adolescent fear period and is neglected can become a lifelong phobia. But by paying careful attention to his emotions while working him slowly, you can make great progress toward eliminating his fear. In fact, after lots of painstaking work, it may seem to disappear as suddenly as it came.

The more you socialize your dog and allow him pleasant experiences, the less likely it is you'll end up with a shy or fearful pet. So the two essentials in working with these problems are, first, never praise or comfort the dog when he is acting out an undesirable behavior and, second, give your dog a rich life, one full of friends of all types and ages and adventures of all kinds.

Fussy Eating, Erratic Appetite

The best way to have a dog who is a good eater is to stick to dog food, to give your dog plenty of exercise and don't feed from the table or add yummy leftovers to his chow.

The good news is that many dogs give up their poor eating habits after adolescence. (If you remember what *you* lived on when you were an adolescent, you may think your dog is doing very well.) Even if you decide to fuss over your dog's food, you can still keep things from getting totally out of hand by drawing the line *somewhere*. Unless you enjoy being held hostage to cooking special soups, staying in the kitchen while your dog eats and letting your dog eat his food out of your hand, you can draw the line at dry dog food mixed, for taste, with a little canned dog food. When your dog sniffs it as if it were poisoned and walks away, put the food in the refrigerator and don't give him anything else until his next meal. He will more than likely only skip one meal once in a while and for an adolescent with an erratic appetite, that's not so terrible. And, if he's getting out to play with his pals in the fresh air, he's less likely to skip any meals.

Just as coming and going in an ordinary, nonhysterical fashion will help prevent a dog from developing separation anxiety, acting unemotional about whether or not your dog eats is definitely the way to go. If you fall apart every time he fails to clean his bowl, he'll milk his advantage to the fullest. So call him to dinner, place his bowl down, tell him "Okay" and go about your business.

During the writing of this book, probably *because* I was writing this book, I got fed up with the way my own adolescent dog, Dexter, was eating, or, more accurately, not eating. Putting down food and, when he rejected it, taking it away, did not work. Some dogs, dogs as stubborn as mine, seem willing to starve to get their way, the exact thing I had always thought a dog would never do. One day it occurred to me that Dexter was willing to go hungry for days when it was *his* decision. I decided to take that decision away from him. I began to feed him dog food mixed with canned food, but only half his regular portion. Now, even when he ate, he was hungry. My decision, not his. Suddenly, there he was, hanging around the kitchen at three in the afternoon, waiting for his dinner. Again, I gave him half a meal. This time he didn't eat it—he gobbled it up. The next day, I gave Dexter a little more at each meal, but not his full portion. By the third day, my dog was eating. Now, if Dexter turns his nose up at a meal, which happens rarely these days, I simply put it away and give him back a small meal at his next regular feeding. If you have a problem eater, you could try this method on him. I hardly *ever* have to make engine noises and zoom little airplanes of dog food into Dexter's mouth nowadays.

The problem with the traditional method for getting fussy dogs to eat may be that very stubborn dogs, once they go off food, are less and less likely to eat as time goes by. It's as if they get out of the habit of eating. And that's scary. Offering small meals keeps the dog eating, keeps him interested in food. As far as I can see here at home, this works (knock wood).

After *almost* all is said and done, Alfred Grossman, my wonderful veterinarian, suggests that, for house-trained dogs, he prefers free feeding with a good quality dry food. This means the dog's food is available all the time and he eats when he pleases, never feeling frantic about when his next meal is arriving and therefore never overeating.

Grooming Problems

When I am asked to work with a problem dog, I always make it a point to look at the dog's nails. If they are not properly cut, I suspect that the owner is not able to do the necessary grooming because the dog is running the show. When you have won your dog's respect, you will be able to clean his ears, brush him, clean his teeth and cut his nails. This fantastic statement is absolutely true!

If you and your dog have not yet made peace about his grooming, start slowly to turn things around. Begin with brushing. Asking your dog to stand, place one hand gently on his chest or belly and brush him in the areas he likes, avoiding the areas that annoy him. Be sure to brush his head, too, taking long strokes from head to tail that pull his energy down and out in a very relaxing way. Once your dog accepts this kind of brushing, add a stroke here and there where he's touchy, for example, hind legs or tail. Praise as you go. Keep the session short and increase the length of time a little bit each session. Soon you will be able to brush your dog anytime you want to.

If your dog is fussy about having his nails cut, first handle his feet during your play sessions and even after brushing him. Praise as you touch, and keep these sessions very brief. You need not handle all four feet each time. Handling one, even between the toes, as you praise, gets the point across. As your dog gets less tense when you handle his feet, help him become accustomed to the nail clipper. Tell him, "Smell it," and praise him. Don't try to use it right away.

After a week of this nice, easy contact, brush your dog, praise him, let him sniff the clipper and clip one toenail, cutting off only the sharp point. Do not try to make up for lost time by making a big cut. If you cut too much, you'll cut the quick. If your dog has clear nails, you can see it. It's the pink area in the center of the nail. Nothing provokes owner guilt faster than seeing a dog's toenail bleed. If you merely cut the point, this will not happen. Praise as you cut—and quit for the day. The next day, do two nails, and two the day after. If this goes well, you may be able to do a whole paw the following day. Praise with each little snip. Reward at the end with some soothing brushing and a fun game.

Dogs don't seem to mind having their teeth brushed as much

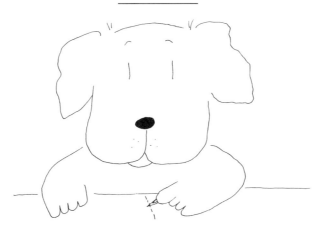

Cut off only the sharp point of the nail.

as you'd think they would. Dexter comes into the bathroom each evening when I am brushing my teeth and waits for me to wet his toothbrush, put on the special dog toothpaste and clean his teeth. Afterward, I let him drink ice-cold water from my hand and he seems very pleased with the whole operation. Just remember, if you are doing a grooming procedure that your dog does not like, there is no law that says you have to do the whole thing at once. Given the chance to adjust in small doses with friendly owner praise, most dogs will learn to tolerate, or even like, most necessities.

When you bathe your dog, let him stand in the dry tub, not in a tub full of water. You'll need a flexible shower hose to do the job easily. Wet him down with warm water. Soap him up carefully with dog shampoo, avoiding not only his eyes but his whole face (that can be done later with a damp washcloth), and once he's clean, rinse with warm water and towel-dry him. This is work, but clean is good. It'll make everyone want to pet your dog more often.

Hormonal Peaks and Valleys, Vacillates Between Dependence and Independence

Remember the ups and downs of adolescence? Now pity your poor dog and try to work with him patiently!

On the days your dog is up, full of beans and full of himself, you need to work at controlling him. This is the perfect day for a lesson, practicing his heeling and some recalls, then a sit-stay and, once back indoors, a long down. You can give him exercise and play some games, too, but make sure you sit on him a little with some training.

On the days your dog seems like a baby puppy again, shy, dependent, not so sure of himself, build his confidence with (you'll never believe this!) some training. Having him heel nicely at your side, doing some recalls and a few stays, with praise for good work, will build him up, make him confident, make him feel terrific. Then you can play his favorite game or take him for a swim or a hike.

When your adolescent dog is one dog on Wednesday and another on Thursday, try to give him the stability of life-as-usual—a little work, a little play, a romp with his friends, some self-control and on to bed.

House Soiling

If your dog is an adolescent, over six months of age, and is still not house trained, there's no time like the present to get the job done. At six months, he is ready to be fully house trained. Once trained, he should even be able to wait all day, if necessary, for you to come home and walk him after work.

Did you crate train your dog? If not, you will have to do so now. See Chapter Four for advice on how to get your dog used to a crate. You will need a humane schedule, a crate and a buzz word for retraining your dog. If you work all day and no one is at home, you may also need someone to walk him—a neighbor, a nice local kid or a professional dog walker—once during the time you are gone.

Your dog will go out first thing in the morning, at some regular time during the afternoon, depending on when the person who will walk him is available, at dinnertime and as late at night as you can manage. It's easiest and best to have your dog sleep in your bedroom with the door closed. If your dog will keep your room clean, he can be out of his crate at night. If he will not, move the crate into your room and close him into it when you go to bed.

The moment you awaken, throw on your jeans or, depending where you live and whom you might run into, toss your coat over your pajamas, open the crate, briefly greet and then leash your dog, and *heel* him out. He's much less likely to have an "accident" if he's working. As he sniffs around for the perfect spot, encourage him with a buzz word. We use hurry up because we live in New York City and other people can hear us. Hurry up not only reminds a distractable dog why he's out, it can communicate clearly to a dog who is on vacation with you that for the next two weeks he must relieve himself on a different surface than he is used to— sand rather than soil or the sidewalk rather than grass. Once your dog has done all he has to do, praise him, bring him in and let him have his freedom, within your eyesight, for an hour or even two.

No one can tell you how long your dog can stay out of the crate without soiling your home. You will have to observe him very carefully in order to make this decision. If it's one hour, after the hour, he goes back into his crate until the next walk. During adolescence, four walks a day should get the job done. Once trained, your dog can do nicely on three walks, as long as at least one of them is a long one or includes a play session in the park.

Suppose your dog does nothing or not enough on his walk. In that case, when you bring him home, he must go right back into the crate. This is how he will learn to pace himself to this humane schedule and not to soil your house. He is unlikely to soil *his* house, the crate, because most dogs, unless taught otherwise by horrible neglect, do not like to be in close proximity to their urine and feces. They prefer more of a hit-and-run procedure, which is why your bedroom is likely to work as a large crate at night.

Did you paper train and is there still newspaper down for your dog to soil? The message to your dog is that it is perfectly acceptable, even laudable, to urinate and defecate indoors. The moment you are ready to begin this house-training program, get rid of the paper. Clean the place where it was, and, if possible, do not allow your dog in that room or area for several weeks. Do not try a little of each, expecting your dog to relieve himself outside when you walk him and indoors on paper when you don't want to, or can't, go out. You will just confuse your dog and accomplish nothing.

House training is a simple, if time-consuming, mechanical job. There is no reason, other than illness, why every dog cannot be trained in a timely fashion to soil out of doors and not on your rugs. Clarity and timing are important. Common sense also helps. For example, if you leave the paper, of course the dog will still use it. You taught him to. If you give your dog food, snacks and water all day long, it will make it much more difficult to house train him. If he eats, he needs to relieve himself. If he noshes all day long, he'll need outings all day long and be difficult to train. Also, while the crate is a terrific tool, leaving your dog crated all day teaches nothing and is terribly cruel.

To review, feed your dog only twice a day, preferably a high-quality food that will produce a good, firm stool. Unless it is truly hot out, do not leave water available all the time. Remove water after dinner. (Once the dog is trained, you can leave water available all the time.) Use a buzz word, such as hurry up, to communicate what you want from your dog. It will also help speed things up on rainy days. Do not let your dog go out in the yard without you to relieve himself while you are training him. You will not know if he did everything. You will not be there to praise him for relieving himself out of doors. And going out alone might encourage stool eating. If you are with him to encourage and praise, the job of house-training will get done more efficiently. Crate your dog until his next walk if he does not relieve himself out of doors. When he does, allow him freedom out of the crate for as much time as he will safely keep the house clean. Increase his time out of the crate as he catches on. Never hit your dog for a house-training accident. Instead, correct him verbally, "No, bad dog. Did you do this?," if you catch him in the act. With a crate, a schedule and you there to monitor the dog, there should be no unobserved accidents.

The dog who is going to be your real best pal must be reliably house trained so that you can take him places with you. Once the job is done, most dogs keep the house clean unless they are ill. You may find one exception here, the dog who marks. Some people consider the dog who marks, that is, the dog who lifts his leg indoors in order to leave his scent, a housebroken dog. I disagree entirely. Though his motive may be different, the problem nonetheless remains. If you have a male dog who hikes his leg indoors, correct him verbally with a booming no, and use the program above to retrain him.

Nota bene: Some dominant females mark like males and if they should do this indoors, they, too, must be taught not to with verbal correction and, if necessary, the use of a crate.

Inability to Resist Temptation

When you are harboring an adolescent delinquent, it is essential that you do not expect of him what you *know* in your heart he can't do. If your dog steals, do not leave him alone with the roast while you run back to the kitchen for the baked potatoes. That is only courting trouble. If he chews, you'll have to put your things too high for him to reach or in the closet with the door closed. If he marks or soils your house, crate him when you cannot watch him. Whatever you do, do not leave the cat to mind the canary and then complain about it later.

In addition to prevention, you'll want to do more than simply wait for your dog to outgrow his problems. Without training, many dogs *never* do. Doing appropriate setups can help correct the problems that concern you.

If your dog is a cookie thief, set out a plate of cookies and sit back and wait. When he goes for the cookies, use the warning *leave it*. But make sure he doesn't get one. If he does, open his mouth and remove it, pronto! If he tries again, correct him with a loud no and, if you are near enough, slip your hand in his collar and give him a shake. Then let him go, sit back again and see what happens.

You can do a setup by dropping a nice, smelly sock on the floor to see if he'll take it and merit an educational correction, too. Almost any failure to resist temptation can be corrected by creating a setup when you are prepared to work with your dog.

With the dog who can resist everything but temptation, be sure to use a leash when out of doors and large doses of prevention at home. When you are with your dog, the warning leave it teaches him what he can think about taking and what he can't. Even practicing his obedience commands in the face of temptation can help somewhat. But when you are not going to be around, you must think ahead and think like a dog. After all, with an adolescent dog, the definition of temptation is broad, rules get forgotten quickly and energy is too high for merely lying around and sleeping all day. Moreover, with a creative teen, just because he has never done something before absolutely does not mean he won't do it now.

Inappropriate Protection

Your dog's protective instincts must be monitored. This is very simple to do, yet many people misunderstand how to handle their dogs' protectiveness and end up accidentally creating aggressive monsters.

It is *not* true that your dog will only protect you if you never let anyone else handle it. Not socializing your dog will create a fearful, abnormal animal who may bite inappropriately. This is not a sound animal capable of good judgment.

When your dog shows any kind of protectiveness, of you or your territory, you must monitor him. If he is acting aggressive now and remains unchecked, he'll be out of control as an adult. Here's how it works. Suppose someone comes to your door. Your dog makes a ruckus. Tell him, "Good dog," for the first bark or two, tell him, "Enough," to quiet him down and ask him to sit and stay while you open the door. Alerting you to the doorbell is all he should be doing.

What about your dog's behavior toward strangers? He should be well mannered, deferential and nonaggressive. He should not bark, growl or lunge at people in the street. If your dog acts this way, correct him with a quick tug on the leash and a deep no. If you got a protective-looking breed, the look of the dog, a Doberman or Shepherd, will protect you in most cases. He need not foam at the mouth to do so. In fact, there's actually nothing scarier than a well-behaved, quiet, big dog. You'd think he was so confident for good reason, wouldn't you? Allowing your dog to bark, growl and lunge, particularly during adolescence, will create an out-of-control, dangerous, inappropriate dog. Innocent people, including your friends and family, are likely to get bitten. *You* may get bitten, too. It is far better to monitor your dog's protectiveness so that it is appropriate and under your control and does not frighten people.

Jumping on People

Jumping up is a tough problem to work with because as you try to convince your adolescent bruiser to keep his big, messy feet off people, half the people he jumps on will be tickled pink that he likes them. Your motivation to correct is for the other half of the population, the ones who are frightened or outraged that your dog has jumped up on them. And the latter half are all lawyers!

Look at it this way. Dogs love to jump up on people. At least half the time, it gets them a lot of petting and attention. It gets the really big dogs close enough to your face to kiss you on the lips. It gets an exciting reaction, whether you like the jumping or not. In order to stop the jumping, you have to spoil the fun of it, and, being a nice guy, you have to find an alternative greeting that the dog will come to like.

When your doorbell rings, do not answer it before putting your dog on-leash. Then open the door, as he starts to jump pull him back with a controlled yank—you do not want to send him flying—and quickly tell him to sit. Now, hand in his collar so that he doesn't pop right back up, pet him and, if the person at your door is willing, have them pet him, too.

Out in the street, of course your dog is on-leash, correct the same way, tug back on the leash, command, "No jumping," then, "Sit." Be sure to praise after he sits. If your dog jumps on you when you come home, first try telling him, "Sit." If that works, praise and work on establishing this new, better habit. If he is wild and jumping and won't listen, you will have to keep a buckle collar on him. Now when you come home and he jumps up, quickly slip your hand under the collar and pull him off and down to the side. Pulling the dog to the side is easier than pulling him straight back, so if you are having trouble with that correction, simply change the direction of your tug.

Correcting jumping is slow work. The people who are delighted when your dog jumps up on them will still want him to do it, thus reinforcing the bad behavior you are trying to stop. You can try to explain to them that you are trying to break your dog of a bad habit, but, believe me, it won't help! They will simply tell you they do not mind when he jumps. So much for help from strangers. Anyway, stick with the program and watch out for the lawyers.

Mounting

Now hear this: It is never acceptable or cute when a dog mounts a person. Mounting is a sexual act. It is also an expression of dominance. When your dog grasps your arm or leg and begins to hump you, he is not telling you he loves you; he is telling you that he views you as a subordinate dog.

You have already been advised to have your dog wear his buckle collar when you are at home with him. Should he begin to mount you, immediately slide your hand into his collar and pull him off, saying no firmly. If he needs additional cooling off, a long down would be just the ticket.

If your dog mounts another dog, he or she (remember, mounting is a way that a dog will show dominance) will usually take care of it, growling or snapping to show displeasure. Unless the dog being mounted is so small that it might get injured or so annoyed that it might begin a fight, you can let the dogs work it out. In case of danger, grasp your dog's collar and quickly take him away.

Some clients have told me that their dogs mount them when they are having sex. Dogs are attracted to the energy and odor of sexual activity and they, indeed, may approach to investigate. A firm no and, if necessary, a firm shove, should end the investigation. Most dogs, thus corrected once or maybe twice, get the point: This is our business, not yours. After that, they can stay in the room and will just curl up, bored, and go to sleep. And three cheers for that!

Obedience Burnout and Selective Deafness

Sometimes during adolescence, dogs seem to hit a learning plateau where they either forget what you taught, do it in a really bored, hangdog way or seem impossible to teach. This is the time to pull back from training and play with your dog. If you teach as you play, all well and good. That happens even if you simply name the elements of the game—find it, take it, catch it, bring it, out, and so forth. After a few weeks, you will be able to return to training with a fresh attitude. Keep lessons short. Have a single goal in mind for each session. When you reach your goal, once, quit, even if you reach it the first time you give that command.

Find it!

Take it!

Catch it!

Bring it!

Out!

Your dog may mimic the way you feel.

With some dogs, you can help yourself and your dog by rereading the dog's standard. Perhaps you can find a better way to integrate that breed's work function into your training program. Or, perhaps your dog needs a way to act out his heritage independent of your training program. Once satisfied, he may be better able to concentrate on obedience work.

Be sure to get positive eye contact. Be sure to keep things clear and simple. Keep your attitude positive as you work. Your dog will tend to mimic the way you feel. Most of all, if your dog seems to be suffering from burnout or has reached a learning plateau, lighten up, invent some active games, make him think as you play, and then resume serious work after this refreshing rest.

Suppose your dog hears everything *but* your plaintive, "Linda, come." Practice watch me. Work your dog on hand signals only, not speaking a word until after the lesson. Try mixing work and games until neither of you can tell one from the other. And, for your dog's sake, when out of doors, use a leash. You hear?

Overexuberance

Your teen will want to do, smell, taste and experience everything. This may mean he's difficult to manage, pulling and darting, wanting into everything he sees. His overexuberance should not be just an annoyance to you, but rather an enthusiasm to be shared and enjoyed. You can calm and tire your dog with exercise or control

Revel in his energy, zest and playfulness.

him with training. When he's too "up" for regular obedience work, you can teach him via active games. But you can also revel in his zest and playfulness. No matter how I feel, I always feel better after a walk with Dexter. So, whenever possible, get with *your dog's* program. Soak it up. Enjoy it.

Pulling

Teaching your dog to heel is your best defense against being pulled down the street. However, there are times when your dog needs to free walk so that he can relieve himself, sniff, check out the local scent scene. If he pulls at these times, times when he's not on command, you can tug and release, reminding him no pulling. You can quickly reverse your direction and give him a taste of his own medicine. This will help until he forgets himself in another minute or so. Or, you can get philosophical about the whole thing, knowing that after exercise and then, finally, after adolescence, he will become mellow enough to walk near you without either having to heel or having to pull. But even then, don't expect him to be perfect.

Separation Anxiety

Most of the dogs I see who are nervous types are not getting enough security from their relationship with their owner. The possibility also exists that the dog is a wreck when you leave because you are not the dog's leader. Look at it this way: if you have won the dog's respect as his leader, then all your decisions are to be trusted, including your decision to leave the house without him. The dog needs to know that your decisions will protect him and not cause him harm. So if you have a problem leaving your dog alone, go back to Chapter Two and practice winning his respect before you do anything else.

The dog who cannot be left alone without having bouts of anxiety often becomes a destructive dog. The advice and information in that section should help with any problems of separation anxiety. In addition, if your dog falls apart when you leave him alone, work slowly and carefully, leaving him for very short periods of time at first and keeping your comings and goings as low key as you can. Do not overpraise him on your return. In fact, it is wise to all but ignore the dog when you first come home and then, a moment later, appear to notice him and say, "Hi." After you check your answering machine, hang up your coat and look through the mail, then greet the dog more warmly, feed him, walk him, play a game when you return.

How is your attitude when you leave your dog alone? Do you fret and worry that he won't be okay? Perhaps his mood is imitating yours, worry and concern rather than confidence and ease. In this case, work on yourself as well as the dog. Few of us can be with our dogs twenty-four hours a day. No dog has to have that much company.

If your dog is having a bad problem with being left, try exercise and a training tune-up, even ten minutes of each, right before you leave. Leave a sterilized bone for him to chew. Leave the radio on to soft music. If your dog really gets hysterical, you may need to crate him to prevent him from hurting himself or trashing your home. In this case, unless he is already crate trained, begin using the crate, minutes at a time, when you *are* home. Do not leave the dog in the crate and leave the house until he accepts the crate with ease.

Slow Learner, Fast Forgetter

When that psychological umbilical cord finally goes, a lot of adolescent dogs seem to lose their motivation to learn. Respond by making and using a plan, working on one thing at a time and doing short, peppy lessons, first indoors, then out. Never work without first getting your dog's attention. Do not ask for repeat after repeat of obedience to a command once your dog has already done it well once. You might be boring him to death. And don't forget to reward your dog with petting and fun games when he's done a decent job. Be sure, too, to recheck your dog's work

Never work without first getting your dog's attention.

function to see if there are any clues to his behavior or misbehavior. In addition, if your dog is an obsessive player and a lackadaisical worker, by all means teach him via games. Practice patience as you go.

Spite

Of the many delightful qualities that bond us to their species, the honesty and openness dogs exhibit may be among the most endearing. If your dog feels sad, angry, playful, silly, or loving, don't you always know it? Spite is a twisted thing, anger turned cold and a desire to get even. This is not the way of dogs. No matter how it looks, your dog, when he appears spiteful, is either anxious or confused. When you walk him for an hour and he waited to get back indoors to use the paper, it's not spite. It's confusion. After all, if the paper you taught him to use is available, what is he *supposed* to assume? Once you are communicating clearly and giving your dog sufficient leadership, education and occupation (work, play and exercise), you should see nothing resembling spite in your house.

Stress Whining

You are waiting to see the veterinarian, eating dinner with company, on the way to dog class, delivering a talk at your local breed club, and your half-grown, half-trained adolescent is whining. He's not looking at you, catching your eye, because he needs a walk, is cold, hasn't been fed. He's just there, hanging around, and this noise, this nonstop, terrible, high-pitched moaning is coming from him, almost as if the sound had nothing to do with the dog. He may whine in dog class while obeying a command. He may whine while chewing a dog toy. He may wake up in the middle of the night and, finding that the lights are off and there's nothing to do, start whining, loud. Congratulations! You've got a stress whiner.

Stress whining is an unconscious activity. This is a most important fact, because when you say no in your best, I-am-alpha-and-you-better-listen-or-else tone, your dog will not have the faintest idea what you're talking about. If you shake him by the collar, send him to his crate, squirt him with a water gun, put him on a long down, he'll still stress whine. None of these corrections will work because he doesn't know he's whining. Think of it this way: Suppose instead of correcting the dog for whining, you praised him when he wasn't whining. That wouldn't work either. How could he understand what he was being praised for? So if the dog is doing something you just can't stand, something comparable to scraping chalk on a blackboard, and he doesn't even know he's doing it, and if the standard, humane corrections and praise that work so well for everything else won't work here, what's a person to do? I was hoping you'd ask!

Step 1: You must make the dog aware of what he is doing. You will get nowhere until you do. Do this by teaching the dog to whine on command. As you teach, the dog will begin to become conscious that he is whining.

Begin by whining with your dog, naming the activity and praising him madly for whining with you. You can start lots of dogs whining by whining. In this case, issue the command cry, whine, sing, whatever you want to call it. (Think ahead to the possibility of tricks when naming this activity.) Begin to whine, repeating the command, "Cry, baby, good baby," as your dog joins in. Work for a few minutes at a time, once or twice a day.

Or, if your dog will not whine with you, in which case, I promise you, you're going to feel mighty silly whining all by yourself, then you must wait for those situations that inspire your dog to whine. When the dog starts this unpleasant serenade, praise, command, praise and whine along.

Initially, temporarily, there's going to be a lot more whining at your house. Yet contrary to appearances, this first step *is* a step in the right direction.

Notice that as soon as you begin to name the activity and praise the dog for whining, a profound change will take place. Remember how the dog whined before, not looking at you? Now he will. When he does, he is already beginning to become conscious of what he is doing. Your whining, an important part of this work, and your naming and praising the activity, make him *see* what he is doing. He sees it in you. You are doing it. And he becomes aware of it because it now has a name and merits reenforcement. Work this way for at least one week.

Step 2: When working with dogs, when you name an activity, you begin to own it. That is, if you can start something (heel, speak, stay, etc.), you can stop it. Now you can get your dog to whine. You whine, you say, "Cry, baby, good baby," and you praise like crazy. Once this is working well, you can begin to call a halt to the whining. First, whine with your dog for a minute or two. (It actually feels nice, doesn't it?) Then say, "Enough," in your serious, alpha voice. *If* your dog has been whining on command and making eye contact while doing so, this will work. Of course, if you are down at his level, moaning and whining, stand up before commanding enough. And if he stops in surprise at your change of tone and heart, it's a fine beginning. Now quickly praise him and to lengthen the time he resists whining, immediately snap on his leash and take him for a nice walk.

As you practice these two steps, you will have more and more control over this activity. Within a few weeks, after diligent practice, you should be able to stop the dog from whining by just saying enough.

Now that you have a little peace and quiet, let's think about why your dog might stress whine. Any dog can do this, but certain breeds and types are more likely to. Some people think these breeds or individuals are "high-strung." I disagree. Stress whining usually occurs in dogs that were bred for really tough work and are not getting the opportunity to do it. Some Nordic dogs, for example, tend to stress whine. So do some Dobermans, Shepherds and Pit Bulls. These are all dogs with enormous energy and very high intelligence. While they all make great pets, they have a very strong need to use themselves. Stress whining can be an urgent message from your dog to you. The message says, "Find me work."

The dog is a very agreeable, adaptable being. You do not have to set out for the Pole with your Malamute or acquire a flock of sheep for your whining Shepherd. But as your work to stop stress whining succeeds—and often this work will end the problem so that in time you will not have to be saying enough—begin to think of ways to work your dog's mind and body that will please both of you—more obedience work, tracking, sled dog racing, nursing home or school visits, jogging, swimming (except for sled dogs), Frisbee, ball playing.

Any stress whiner can happily reform—with a little bit of work to make him conscious of his habit and with challenges and accomplishments to satisfy both his intelligence and his physical being.

Unreliable

Until your dog is well trained enough and mature enough to be trustworthy, when you are out of doors and there is no fence, use a leash. Period.

Wildness

Most adolescent dogs spend at least some of their time acting like maniacs. This behavior may be an outlet for a great spurt of energy or a response to great joy. Dogs do not talk about their feelings. They act them out. So when you come home tired and your dog tears through the house like the 4:02 Westbound, it just means he's full of energy from sitting around all day with nothing to do and he's also beside himself with joy at your arrival home.

There are two "cures" for wildness. First, exercise your dog. He needs it desperately and you will not be able to contain him unless he has an outlet for his energy. Second, if your dog is getting good regular exercise and still acts wild, particularly when you need him not to—he's with you in a store or you are on the phone—you will have to use an obedience command, preferably the down-stay, to gain some control. Use an obedience command? What a concept! You would be surprised at the number of people who train their dogs and don't *use* the commands that would help them live sanely with their pets. That is what obedience training is for.

Of course, your adolescent dog won't quit being wild totally. Perhaps you need to accept some of his wild behavior, when and where you can, as zest. Wildness sounds bad. Zest sounds good. Sometimes a little word play is in order; that doesn't change the dog's behavior but rather your view of it. If no harm is being done, why not, at least for part of the time, think *zest* instead of *wildness*. You might actually enjoy watching your dog race through the house in order to express his boundless joy at your return from the mailbox. After all, who else treats you that way?

A Special Problem

Sometimes what looks like many problems may be only one. When problems don't get solved even though they seem annoying to you, they may be serving a deeper need than what appears on the surface, a need you may not even know you have. In some cases, people unconsciously set up a kind of codependency relationship with their dog. When this is the case, until that is resolved, it is nearly impossible to correct the specific dog problems that result.

In order to raise and train a dog appropriately, you must see yourself and the dog as two independent creatures. Though the heart may embrace the dog fully, one's image of oneself must be apart from that of the dog. When the dog seems so much a part of the owner that he or she can't take any criticism of the dog, this is a sign of trouble. If your self-image is intertwined with that of the dog, you will not be able to correct the dog, leave him alone without projecting hysteria to him, let him be his own dog. You may even need the complete focus the dog problems require of you in order to distract yourself from worse worries. These kinds of problems cannot be solved by dog trainers. In such cases, the owner will need to resolve personal problems before being able to resolve dog problems.

Because they are so malleable, dogs can easily be unintentionally worked into codependency relationships. This is food for thought if no matter what you do, your dog problems seem to remain or if you've had the same problems repeatedly with several dogs. But remember that, like dogs, humans are lifelong learners, capable of astonishing recovery. If you suspect that this scenario may describe your problems with your dog, it shouldn't cause you grief. Once you work through your problems, you'll be able to work through your dog's problems, too.

The Last Word in Dog Training

If you sometimes wish for an easier dog or the kind of quick fix that requires a wonderful insight and no subsequent follow-up work, remember that the slow fix has many rewards. During the time you spend training your dog, you will do much more than educate him. You will also learn *from* him, and grow to appreciate him more than you possibly could without this time and attention. As your dog learns to respond to you, as he reveals his quick mind and his sense of humor and as he comes to respect you as his leader, the bond between you will grow and grow. Graceful, mutual education between master and dog can and should be a pleasure as long as he lives.

Part Four

"My favorite thing is to go where
I've never been."

DIANE ARBUS

10

BUILDING THE DOG
YOU WANT

I think of dogs as inside dogs and outside dogs. The inside dog is one who shares his charms within the family. You love and adore him, but other people do not see or feel what is extraordinary about him. In other words, he is an introvert of sorts. The outside dog is the extrovert. He displays his charms to the world. Of course, he loves you best. But he can fool strangers into thinking he loves *them* best. He thrives on attention from any nice person. In fact, he solicits it. He is great in a crowd. He can do demos at the mall or for schoolchildren. He could be a model, an actor, a dog about town. You can't get down the block with him without adding new members to his fan club.

Not every dog is a born extrovert, and some, no matter what you do, will never cultivate an interest in a wide circle of people.

But if the dog of your dreams is an outside dog, even if the dog you own is not, you can increase his social skills and add immeasurably to the pleasure he gives you and others as well.

Your ideal dog doesn't just happen. He needs to be built, slowly, patiently, intelligently, with humor. If you want him to be the best, you have to make him the best with careful planning, devotion, time. Even a puppy who is extraordinarily outgoing, lively and people-oriented, can lose those very positive qualities if he is left uneducated, underexercised and unsocialized. So if what you really want is a dog everyone will love, one full of fun and humor, one who can go anyplace with you, one who will love just about any dog or person he meets, you'll need to supersocialize him, making him your sidekick and taking him everywhere you can.

The dog who is going to *be* more, *needs* more. He needs a wide variety of experiences, most of them *away from home*, so that he will be able to face with equanimity anything that might come his way. When my special friend, Oliver, a Golden Retriever, met a Chimp on roller skates at Bloomingdales, Ollie wagged his tail. When the Chimp took hold of his leash and began to skate down the aisle, Oliver heeled along at his side. That's equanimity! If that's the kind of fun you'd like to have with your special friend, here are some ideas to help make him the kind of fun dog for whom whatever monkey holds the leash is alpha.

COMMUNICATE WITH YOUR DOG ON A REGULAR BASIS Some people think of communicating with their dogs only when issuing a command or a reprimand. But if you want to build a better dog, you must think of him as someone you communicate with more frequently.

I remember going to a dog show years ago with Captain Arthur Haggerty, the trainer who had been my idol when I first got into the business, and still is. His Golden Retriever, Muffin, was in the car and as we got out, he told her, "Stay in the car." I began to laugh. "I thought I was the only one who did that!" I said, believing until that moment that no one else communicated with a dog that way. Naturally, the dog had no choice. With the windows just opened for air and the door locked, how could she do other than stay in the car? But that's human logic. Dog logic is different. Telling the dog to stay in the car was showing her that she wasn't

Communicate with your dog on a regular basis.

forgotten by accident. It let her know, since we obviously remembered she was there, that we would return. This allowed Muffin to wait in the car without getting anxious. This kind of communication is an important step in building a better dog.

If you communicate simply with your dog, he or she will learn to listen better and to understand more than just a set of commands. From the simple courtesy of saying heel when you are changing your position in obedience class—most people asked to face another way just drag their dogs with them—to the additional consideration of saying wait while waiting at the curb with your dog for a light to change, the addition of short sentences, used consistently, makes the dog a more discriminating listener and a better, more interesting friend.

SHARE ADVENTURES   Don't just let your dog out in the yard or walk him around the block when there are lots of places you're going anyway where he could accompany you. The dog is a born sidekick. He's never too busy or too tired to go along whenever and wherever you choose. By including him in on your life, you calm him, bond to him, exercise him and educate him, with very little extra effort on your part.

Once he's got some manners, you can take your dog with you when you go visiting and on errands. Let him meet all kinds of children and adults, have him play with other dogs, and in doing so, teach him to be confident.

The better he's trained, the more freedom you can give him, the more places you can go, the more appropriate and less embarrassing he'll be. People sometimes think training takes away a dog's freedom. On the contrary, it is your dog's good behavior that lets you take your dog into stores, visiting, anywhere at all. It is reliable training that allows you, when appropriate and legal, to take off the leash and let your dog run about or play with other dogs. It is reliable training that will help your adolescent dog become the dog you want him to be and allow you to take him on what for you might be little outings but for him will be grand adventures. He's a dog, isn't he? Even a walk to the bank can make his spirits soar.

Is your dog friendly and does he enjoy meeting new people? In other words, is he an inside dog or an outside dog? Since each breed writes its own definition of friendly, you must know your breed. The German Shepherd is rarely as promiscuous as the Golden Retriever in sharing its affection. No matter. Any dog can give and get pleasure from the experience of meeting new people if the situation is handled in a way that suits the kind of dog you have. Reasonable expectations are in order here as in all matters concerning your dog. The Golden may just sit and wallow in petting, from anyone. The Shepherd may thrill a child by obeying a series of commands and then receiving praise for working.

Never be afraid to let other *nice* people pet your dog or even work him, as long as you hand over the leash and tell your dog "Okay." If instead of letting your dog socialize, you pull him away from people in the hope that it will make him more protective, you will end up not with a protector but with a grouchy, unsocialized dog. For most people, a friendly dog is the best bet, but you don't have to let your dog socialize with people *you* wouldn't socialize with. Saying no puts you in the role of protector of your dog, a role you took on when you first acquired him. As you begin to take your terrific teen on little daily adventures—and on occasional grand adventures—you'll find that, introvert or extrovert, he'll become more sociable and friendly as he gets more pleasant experiences in the larger world.

We decided to go on a grand adventure when Dexter was ten months old. We took our tired selves and both dogs on a swimming vacation in Vermont. This was the sort of journey where you pack your dogs and your belongings in your car and head for a place far more relaxing than the one you're in, *and* it was another kind of trip as well. This was a journey to nourish the mind and the soul. Away from home with our dogs, we got to know them better, to admire and enjoy them more. As it turned out, this was Scarlet's last vacation, since, too sad to say, we lost her the following January. But on our last day at the lake, she took a spectacular dive off the pier to join Steve in the water. It is how I most like to picture her now. She always was a go-big-or-stay-home type of dog.

The dog who shares your adventures is more likely to teach you and surprise you for all her life. Just remember, for now, when you travel with your adolescent dog, that no matter how well you feel you know him, he is in the process of changing. So the dog you load into the car along with your bathing suits and paperback mysteries may not be the same dog who emerges from the car when you reach your destination. Keep in mind that during your dog's adolescence, the fact that he has never done something before is virtually meaningless in predicting future behavior. Adolescence is a time of trial and error—mostly error. And the little dog who always came when called can take off rapidly and without warning when he sees his first rabbit, when he is off-leash in an open area, when another dog appears to woo him away, when the mood strikes him to stretch his legs and explore, to be daring or naughty, to see what's there, or what isn't there. As a teenager, he's constantly testing the boundaries of his world. This means he is not to be trusted unattended. It also means you'll have more fun and more laughs on your vacation than if you left him in a kennel. Watching your dog swim for the first time, chase a frog, explore the woods and make new friends can make the world fresh and new for you too.

DOLL HIM UP If you want your dog to enjoy people, it is your job to help him be as attractive as possible so that people will want to stop and pet him. Keep him clean and well brushed. Keep his nails cut short and smooth so that he doesn't accidentally scratch anyone when he slaps his paw into their hand. If your dog has a face only you and his mother could love, put a big ribbon on his neck and tie it with a gigantic bow. The more your dog learns to love people, the more charming he'll become. There's really no such thing as a well-socialized, well-trained, well-groomed dog who is not appealing to dog lovers, especially when the dog is wearing an oversized bow! The bow, by the way, works wonders in helping you to socialize a scary-looking breed. A Rottweiler with a big bow on his collar is simply no longer a scary-looking dog.

MAKE HIM STEADY AS A ROCK   Your dog should be predictable. If you don't know how your dog will behave in the obedience ring, the mall, the nursing home, he's not ready to go to places like that. Start small, a new friend at a time. Make sure he can hold a sit-stay while being petted. Many a good tooth has been chipped by a nice dog popping up to give a kiss in the middle of getting petted. So, socialize as you go, keep training response tight and build up to your talk for schoolchildren or your visit to the mall with Fido in tow.

BRING OUT HIS HUMOR   Does your dog have a funny bone? Good. Encourage it. Teach him a funny trick or two. I've never met the person too sophisticated to enjoy a silly dog trick. And laughter can break the ice in nearly any situation, giving your dog as much pleasure as you and others glean from the experience.

My Golden, Ollie, knew a lot of tricks and I gave a lot of talks and demos with him. On one occasion, he apparently found my presentation too serious and he began to do some tricks on his own. When the audience got hysterical, I probably turned beet-red, figuring I had done something stupid I wasn't aware of. But then I looked down at my side and saw my dog sitting high and beaming at the laughter. He might as well have said, "*This* is the way to do a talk, Ma!"

When choosing tricks, pick the ones that are appropriate for your breed, his size, his structure, but do not worry about your dog's sense of dignity. I never met a dog who didn't love to make people laugh.

Bring out his humor.

KEEP HIM FIT   The dog of your dreams is not an overweight couch potato, is he? He should be in tip-top shape. Your adolescent pal needs high energy and the shine on his coat that good health and a superior diet will give him. Exercise will give him stamina, too. More than that, it gives him a constructive outlet for his great energy. And, lest you forget, a tired teen is a good teen. That fact can't be repeated too often!

THINK: SAFETY FIRST!   As you supersocialize your best friend, never forget that he's an unreliable teenager. Just because he's never done a thing before does *not* mean he won't do it this time. So, use your leash and use common sense. As you drive to an adventure, make sure the car window is not open so far that your dog could jump out. Adolescents get crazy ideas sometimes. Check your dog's collar and leash to make sure neither is worn and about to tear. Never, even on a quick stop, leave your dog alone in the car in hot weather or tie him up outside a store. A car can heat up in minutes, creating a lethal atmosphere for a dog. And your dog, tied up outside a store, can tempt a thief.

The more you take your dog with you, the more his safety will become second nature to you, leaving you free to concentrate on the fun of his company.

Treat him with respect. After all, having a dog is a blessing.

TREAT HIM WITH RESPECT   You needn't worry about your dog losing respect if he does an adorable barking trick or rolls over and pretends to sleep. Treating him with respect means understanding he's a dog and he's in your care. Legally, he has few rights. He counts on you for the consideration and protection he needs. So while you're out there giving him the time of his life, building the dog you want, you also have to make sure no one teases him, overtires him or makes fun of him. He needs to be treated with the dignity his species deserves. For that he counts on you.

For protection, he *counts on* you.

HAVE TWO ACES UP YOUR SLEEVE Two easy commands will help immeasurably when you are out and about, socializing your dog and having grand adventures. The first, wag your tail, helps your dog instantly project his friendliness and his humor. Teach it by tone of voice alone. Ask your dog to stand and stay. Now bend a little and smile, saying in your friendliest voice, "Wag your tail, *good* dog, wag your tail." Done!

The second ace up your sleeve is *kiss* and this adorable "trick" has a serious flip side. The forgetful adolescent dog who escalates happiness into wildness at the drop of a "Good dog!" can be reminded how to behave when asked to give someone a kiss. After all, he's going to know what kiss means, a lick on the mouth, cheek or hand, depending upon how you teach it. Therefore, kiss does *not* mean leap on the person petting you and knock them flat.

Teaching a dog to kiss on the lips is easy. Say, "Kiss, good dog, kiss," and, first slurping your tongue noisily for a second, kiss him smack on his mouth. With a little practice, you've got a charming trick. Do I need to tell you not to do this with aggressive dogs? Okay. Don't teach this trick to any dog who is not certifiably gentle.

What if the thought of kissing dog lips makes you want to shout, "Oooo! Germs!" You'd sooner catch a disease from kissing a human than a dog, but there's no arguing taste. So if you want a kiss, but not on the lips, take a little dab of butter, put it on your cheek or on the back of your hand, command sweetly, "Kiss." Practice. Done.

Kiss!

Good dog!

TUNE UP THAT TRAINING　For an adolescent dog, for safety's sake, always work at keeping training tight and enthusiasm high. The best way to do this is to give your dog little training tune-ups periodically. Even your tune-up can be an adventure, done in a new place, done in a new way. For dogs this age the world is so intensely interesting that concentration time is short. You can do fun lessons by taking your dog to a new place and interspersing short work sessions with long periods of exploration. Underlying the lesson, heeling or recalls or whatever, your dog is learning that he must obey whenever you ask him to. In a way, working in short spurts is more realistic and more consonant with the way you'll treat him at home. And your dog will be having fun as he learns.

BUILD YOUR DOG'S CONFIDENCE　Interesting, happy experiences and lots of appropriate positive reenforcement build confidence in a dog. Whenever possible, every day if I can, I try to think of an adventure for Dexter, a new place to go, new experiences for him to try, something new to learn, lots of praise to help him feel accomplished and polished, sure of himself, interested in the world. Games build confidence, too, especially those that reenforce good training while allowing for lots of exuberance. A super game for teenaged dogs is the group recall. Use one or more extra people to call the dog back and forth. Go for speed. Praise like crazy. Let the pauses be brief and send the dog running quickly to the next person. If your dog's interest flags, use a squeak toy, a whistle, a favorite ball. Be inventive and keep it fun.

Another important game for adolescent dogs is come, don't come. Work with one of your dog's friends, putting both dogs on a sit-stay. Next, call one of the dogs, using his name and the command come. If both dogs come, correct the dog whose name was not called. In a short amount of time, both dogs will have learned to listen better. Instead of half-listening and running in because they see the other dog doing it, they will *really* pay attention, listening for and waiting for their own name before they go.

Go big, or stay home.

Having a Dog Is a Howl

Ever since I was a child, I wanted a dog with whom I could howl. I first found that dog in Scarlet. Shepherds, like wolves, are natural howlers, so it was no surprise that when I howled Scarlet quickly joined me. What was a surprise was to see firsthand that any dog can learn to howl. When Scarlet was one year old, I taught an obedience class in our local park. At the end of every session, dogs and humans alike would indulge in a group howl before parting. I have read many theories on what it means when wolves howl, many ideas about why they do it. If you are intrigued, and if, like me, you'd like to howl with your adolescent dog, just do it. When you are really into your howling, you will no longer need someone else to tell you why wolves howl. When Dexter and I want to express our deepest feelings in their purest form, we get together and have a good howl. This is the cement I need with *each* dog of my dreams.

Each dog you live with can be the dog of your dreams, as long as you give him the time and love that relationship requires. Building the dog you want is not something to be accomplished quickly or in a set amount of time. It is a lifelong project, an integral part of the way you and your dog relate to each other, ever learning, ever growing, ever increasing the love and respect you feel for one another.

When you think of how to raise and love your dog, take a page from Scarlet's book, go big, or stay home. I promise you, you'll have no regrets.

INDEX

ISBN 0-87605-742-3